CHER HAMPTON

The Somatic Therapy Handbook

Self-Soothing Techniques for Healing Trauma, Enhancing the Mind-Body Connection, and Stress Relief

Contents

BONUS: Your Free Gift

I'm only offering this bonus for FREE to my readers. This is a way of saying thanks for your purchase. In this gift, you will find a course with extra tools to start your inner journey.

The Personality Development Wisdom Course

Master the Art of Becoming the Best Version of Yourself for Ultimate Succes and Growth!

Inside this course, you will find:

1. Personality Development - An Overview
2. How to Transform Yourself into a Better Version
3. How To Improve Your Body Language
4. How to Boost Up Your Self-Confidence, Self-Esteem, and Motivation
5. Best Tips to Overcome Procrastination
6. The Power of Positive Thinking
7. How to Improve Your Workplace Wellness
8. How to Enhance Your Softskill
9. Learn and Practice the Art of Work-Life Balance
10. How to Deal With Failures
11. How to Manage and Overcome Your Fears
12. Best Ways to Deal With Difficult People
13. Stress and Energy Management
14. How to Have a Productive Day
15. Bonus 1 - Cheat Sheet
16. Bonus 2 - Mind Map
17. Bonus 3 - Top Resource Report
18. Bonus 4 - 10 Extra Articles

To receive this extra **bonus,** go to: https://booksforbetterlife.com/somatic-therapy-handbook

Or scan the QR code:

Introduction

"Before there are words, there is the wordless communication of the body."

— MICHAEL CHANGARIS

Healing is gardening work—a lot like tending to a beautiful yet overgrown garden. Imagine this garden has been neglected for years. Weeds have sprouted everywhere, choking the life out of once-vibrant flowers. Thorny bushes have invaded, and a thick layer of leaves covers the once-fertile soil. The entire ecosystem is out of balance, and the garden's natural beauty is hidden beneath the chaos.

Like this garden, our emotional landscape can become overgrown and tangled. Past traumas, unresolved feelings, and negative beliefs can sprout like weeds, choking out the aspects of our lives that feel like light and life. We may feel overwhelmed, stuck, or lost within our own emotional wilderness. However, just as a skilled gardener can restore a neglected garden to its former glory, we too can embark on a journey of emotional healing.

You see, I have learned and experienced a lot about healing throughout my own journey; the fact that it is as messy as it is a beautiful process. The fact that it will barely make sense on some, well, most days.

Sometimes it'll feel a lot like you're taking more steps back than you are taking steps forward, but the most critical thing that it has taught me is that healing is rarely ever about maintaining a sense of calm but rather about maintaining our sense of choice.

It's so much more than being in a constant state of Zen the whole time. It's about immersing ourselves in experiences and activities that can help us cultivate inner peace and a sense of well-being, learning to identify and address the root causes of our emotional pain. This can look a lot like delving into past traumas, examining the beliefs we were conditioned to believe in, and those patterns preventing us from becoming the best versions of ourselves. Is it easy? No. Many people I have encountered and interacted with have said: "Well, I don't see any point in doing all this therapy, healing, or inner work. You can't change the past. You can't change what happened."

That's true, we can't change what happened to us, but we can change how those experiences affect us now.

To heal your trauma does not mean you need to "get over" what happened. To heal does not mean that you have to forget what happened. Healing does not mean you won't ever get triggered again or have those big, messy feelings that come with a messy past. Healing doesn't mean you won't ever dissociate, panic, or experience pain over what happened.

It's none of those things. It is, however, choosing to work with our stories as self-empowerment agents so that they don't, at a later stage, turn and work against us. It's about plucking out the weeds and leaving enough room for the vibrant colors of joy, gratitude, and self-acceptance to shine through. It's how we transform that chaotic and overgrown inner world into a haven of serenity, nourishment, and beauty.

Our thoughts and emotions can greatly affect our physical well-being and vice versa. This is why many experts believe that healing is best achieved through an integrated approach that considers both the psychological and physiological aspects of a person's health.

One type of therapy that embodies this integrated approach is somatic therapy. Somatic therapy is based on the belief that our bodies hold onto memories, emotions, and stress that can contribute to mental and physical health problems. By focusing on the body and its sensations, somatic therapy aims to help people release trapped energy and emotions and ultimately achieve a greater sense of well-being.

Somatic therapy uses a variety of techniques to help us become more aware of our bodies and the physical sensations they experience. These techniques may include breathing exercises, movement practices, meditation, and other mindfulness-based practices. By increasing awareness of the body and its sensations, people can learn to regulate their emotions better and manage stress.

One of the greatest benefits of somatic therapy is that it can be effective in treating a range of mental health conditions. For example, somatic therapy has been shown to be helpful in the treatment of anxiety disorders, depression, PTSD, and other trauma-related conditions. By addressing the physiological aspects of these conditions, somatic therapy can help people feel more in control of their emotions and less reactive to triggers.

Another benefit of somatic therapy is that it can promote greater self-awareness and insight. By learning to tune into our bodies and physical sensations, people can better understand how their thoughts and emotions affect their overall well-being. This increased self-awareness can be empowering, as it allows us to take a more active role in our own healing process.

Our bodies and our minds are intricately intertwined. More so than we think. Without realizing it, trauma can get trapped in parts of our body and manifest physically. By bringing awareness to these sensations and learning how to work with them, we can begin to heal on a deeper level. This book is your roadmap toward healing through somatic therapy. We will discover how to tap into the wisdom of our bodies to release trauma, tension, and stress. It's going to help us find the path to healing and create a sense of wholeness within ourselves. It's the first step toward healthier, happier, more integrated versions of ourselves. Let's dive right into it.

1

What is Somatic therapy

"Our bodies tell us truths which are much harder for our thoughts and emotions to access."

— UNKNOWN

Something that most of us aren't willing to admit is that we are not in any way or form connected to our bodies. We've learned or conditioned ourselves to retreat to our thoughts, cognitive awareness, or our own intellectual insights to navigate dysregulation. In a way, you can think of it in this way: the bigger the emotions we feel, the more we think and tune into our thoughts. That is until we hit a wall. We become stuck and realize that all the thinking is actually not doing much for us. It isn't regulating our nervous systems or the chaos that we feel inside our bodies. When we hit this wall, it's an invitation to rebuild that body-mind connection. It's an opportunity to turn inward with compassion, care, curiosity, and conscious intention. This is somatic therapy at heart. Or what I like to call the feel, process, and release method.

Somatic therapy is a type of therapy that focuses on building the relationship between the mind and the body. It is rooted in the idea that our emotions and experiences are not just in our heads but are also stored in our bodies. In learning to understand and work with these physical sensations, it can help individuals heal from a range of emotional and psychological traumas.

The word "somatic" is derived from the Greek word "soma," which means "body." In somatic therapy, we use a variety of techniques to help us become more aware of our physical sensations and how they relate to our emotional experiences.

The one thing that we should understand is that the body has its own innate wisdom and ability to heal. By bringing attention to the physical sensations of the body, we can access this wisdom and work through emotional and psychological issues in a holistic way.

The Principles of Somatic Therapy

Somatic work is a lot of things. If you think about it, it's in that very same breath that you're taking right now. It's in those moments when you take your hand, put it on your chest, and say hello to yourself. It's being within yourself-even if it's just for a split second. This is what helps us foster a deeper understanding of ourselves and cultivates greater self-awareness and resilience. It's what empowers us to explore and connect with our bodies to promote that overall sense of well-being and to build a more fulfilling life. But to get there, we have to understand the principles that will enable us to put them into practice.

The Marvel of Our Makeup: Understanding Our Bodily Symphony and the Rhythm of Stress

I want you to think of your body as a complex symphony orchestra, each part playing a crucial role in creating a harmonious melody. Imagine the cells as musicians, tissues as sections of the orchestra, and organs as different instrumental families, all conducted by the nervous system, our very own maestro.

Now, did you know we have not one but two nervous systems? Yes! Our bodies are a two-for-one deal. We have the central nervous system, consisting of the brain and spinal cord, which is like the conductor of the orchestra. It makes big decisions, interprets the music (or in this case, the world around us), and guides the body's responses.

Then we have the peripheral nervous system, the diligent orchestra members carrying out the maestro's instructions. It connects the central nervous system to the rest of the body, making sure every toe tap and finger flick happens at the right moment. This system is further divided into the somatic nervous system, controlling voluntary actions, and the autonomic nervous system, taking care of the involuntary stuff like your heartbeat and digestion.

But there's more! The autonomic system itself has two subdivisions: the sympathetic and the parasympathetic. Think of them as two talented soloists with very different styles. The sympathetic system is the passionate, intense virtuoso, preparing your body for action during times of stress (the "fight-or-flight" response). This is the system that makes your heart pound when you're startled, and your palms sweat when you're nervous. Its purpose? To keep you safe and ready to respond to any threats.

3

On the other hand, the parasympathetic system is like a soothing lullaby singer, helping your body relax and recover (the "rest and digest" response). It slows the heart rate, aids digestion, and promotes a state of calm. Its role? To conserve energy and maintain a state of equilibrium.

Stress is like the uninvited guest at our orchestra's performance. A little bit of it can keep the performance lively and the musicians on their toes. But too much? That's when the beautifully coordinated concert starts to feel more like a chaotic jam session. Chronic stress keeps the sympathetic system in overdrive like a violinist playing at prestissimo (very fast) tempo non-stop. This can lead to health issues like high blood pressure, anxiety, and digestive problems.

Just as a finely tuned orchestra can adapt to a change in rhythm or an unexpected solo, so can our bodies. Through practices like somatic therapy, we learn to understand our bodies' responses to stress better, heal from its impacts, and even change our bodily 'tune' to one that promotes resilience and harmony.

The Body Holds Trauma and Emotional Pain

The human body is a complex and amazing system that is capable of incredible things. However, it is not immune to the effects of trauma and emotional pain. In fact, the body has an incredible ability to store these experiences and hold onto them over time. Think of it like a sponge. When it is exposed to water, it absorbs it and begins to expand, but when we wring it out, all the water is released, and it goes back to its original size. Let's say you've experienced emotional trauma, just like how the water would fill the sponge up; these experiences can fill up and occupy space inside of our bodies. The body may tighten and hold onto this pain.

This is where the principle of somatic therapy would come in, the idea that working with the body and not against it can help us release these experiences and promote healing.

You see, when we experience traumatic events, the body responds in a number of ways. The fight-or-flight response can be activated, which floods the body with adrenaline and cortisol, preparing it to respond to the threat. Physical changes may also occur, which could look a lot like increased heart rate, rapid breathing, and muscle tension. All of these are changes designed to help the body survive the threat, but they can also result in physical sensations that persist long after the event has passed.

Over time, these physical sensations can become chronic, leading to symptoms such as chronic pain, fatigue, and even autoimmune disorders. This is because the body has not been able to release the trauma and emotional pain that is stored within it. Somatic therapy recognizes that addressing these issues is what can help us move past them and move our lives in the direction that we want them to.

The Mind and Body are Interconnected

The mental and physical aspects of our being are not separate but in fact are a single entity. When looking at it from a scientific point of view, this interconnectedness can be seen in the ways through which our mental well-being often affects our physical health, for example, stress. Research has shown time and time again that negative emotions tend to have a detrimental effect on our immune system, while positive emotions, like joy, excitement, and contentment, have a much more protective effect and promote immune function and lower our risk of chronic illness.

In addition to these physiological connections, there are also social factors that we need to take into consideration. For instance, our thoughts and belief systems can have a very powerful impact on our physical health because they influence everything around us. From our ability to heal from illness to the perception that we have of pain. On that same note as well, the support that we receive from the community of people around us can also contribute to our health in a meaningful way.

Somatic therapy recognizes and acknowledges that although this interconnectedness might be complex and multifaceted, taking the steps we need to weave that thread in between can help us achieve a greater sense of vitality in our lives.

The Body Has Innate Wisdom and the Capacity for Healing

Just as a gardener tends to the soil and plants in their garden, our bodies, too, possess a miraculous ability to heal and renew themselves. This innate wisdom of the body is a symphony of complex biological processes and natural mechanisms that work in harmony to maintain our well-being. Consider, for a moment, the marvel of our immune system, the body's first line of defense against foreign invaders. Composed of an intricate network of cells, proteins, and organs, the immune system is a silent guardian that works tirelessly to protect us from infections, diseases, and other harmful substances. This remarkable system not only identifies and neutralizes pathogens but also remembers previous encounters, allowing it to mount a swifter and more effective response should the same threat reappear. It is a testament to our body's innate wisdom that we are able to adapt and become more resilient in the face of ever-changing challenges.

Have you ever stopped to wonder how a simple cut or scrape on your skin miraculously heals itself? This process, known as wound healing, is a complex orchestration of cellular activity that involves inflammation, tissue formation, and remodeling. In a well-choreographed dance, our body's cells work together to rebuild, restore, and revitalize the affected area, all without any conscious effort on our part.

Our emotions and mental state have a profound influence on our body's ability to heal, too. We should never underestimate the power of the mind-body connection.

Oh, and let's not forget about its remarkable ability to detoxify and eliminate harmful substances. Our livers, kidneys, lungs, and skin all play a crucial role in ridding the body of toxins and maintaining internal balance. Through intricate biochemical processes, these organs work hand-in-hand to ensure that we are protected from the harmful effects of environmental pollutants, metabolic waste, and other unwanted substances.

Somatic therapy in this sense recognizes that the wisdom that our bodies carry can help us take a more holistic and empowered approach in healing and unlearning. By focusing on nourishing our bodies and nourishing them through healthy habits, we can continue to tap into the vast reservoir of inner wisdom to promote our own self-healing. The body is, in many ways, a remarkable vessel of healing and transformation.

The Importance Of Self-Awareness and Body-Centered Healing

As humans, we are blessed and gifted with the power of choice. We can choose to ignore, to disconnect, resist or beat ourselves up for simply being human and being capable of feeling the complex emotions that humans are capable of feeling, or we can choose curiosity. We can choose to notice sensations when they arise and facilitate the movement of these feelings by allowing them to exist. That seems like a more attractive option because our quality of life improves in the most magnificent of ways when we choose to change how we relate to our feelings. Is it easy? No, it's not, but worth it, it is.

I wasn't always as self-aware as I am today. Honestly, I wasn't always willing or wanting to do the work. I was afraid of what I would find. More so, I was afraid that I wouldn't like what I found, but as I look back on the journey, I'm glad that I did the work that was required because if I hadn't, I wouldn't be able to share the wisdom and shed light on the things that I have learned about self-acceptance over the years:

- It starts within, a process that begins with understanding our thoughts, feelings, and actions. You see, we are inherently emotional beings. We experience the world through our emotions. It's what keeps us connected to those around us; they keep us alive. Self-awareness helps us to navigate through them successfully, especially the most difficult ones. It teaches us how to properly be with them, not just to think them away.
- It's a vulnerable process. It's about growing the courage to be honest with ourselves about our strengths and weaknesses and willingness to do the work that is necessary for progress.

- It's a special kind of presence, being present in the moment and connecting with the very essence of who we are.
- Self-awareness is communicative—it's being brave enough to ask others for their perspective.
- It's understanding that our individual quirks and traits can help us better navigate the complex relationships in our personal and professional lives.
- It's an openness to change—self-awareness requires a willingness to grow and adapt as you learn more about yourself.
- It's taking time to reflect on our experiences because those are ultimately the biggest reasons why we are the way we are.
- It is a journey that requires patience and compassion as we unpack the layers of what it means to be human.

Self-awareness is not an easy state to get to. Understandably so because it requires us to confront our own thoughts, emotions, and beliefs, which can be uncomfortable and even painful at times; that's why it's natural to want to avoid discomfort by distracting ourselves with external stimuli like social media, television, or work, rather than turning inward to reflect on our inner world.

It also requires us to be honest with ourselves about our flaws and weaknesses, which can be intimidating because what if we are judged or rejected by others? Then there's the culture we live in as well. External success and achievement are much more valued over introspection and self-reflection. We are taught to measure our worth by our accomplishments rather than by inner qualities like empathy and compassion. Our traumas and difficult life experiences have left us feeling disconnected from our emotions and physical sensations. This disconnection can make it challenging to build a healthier relationship with ourselves because we may not even be aware of what we are feeling,

THE SOMATIC THERAPY HANDBOOK

what we need, or how our body is responding to different situations.

Despite how hard it may be, it's a necessary tool for personal growth and transformation. Particularly so in body-centered healing. You see, self-awareness is the ability to understand and recognize our own thoughts, emotions, and physical sensations in the present moment. It allows us to observe how we respond to different stimuli and situations, whether positive or negative, and to recognize patterns in our behavior. In body-centered healing, it helps us connect the dots between the disconnect from ourselves by identifying the root causes of our physical and emotional pain.

When we are self-aware, we are able to recognize and acknowledge how our thoughts, beliefs, and behaviors impact our physical bodies. We learn to notice how we hold tension, where we feel pain, and how our emotions manifest themselves as a physical sensation. This awareness helps us identify and release the underlying emotional and psychological patterns that may contribute to our physical symptoms.

If we are experiencing chronic back pain, for example, self-awareness can help us identify the emotional stressors that may be contributing to the pain. We may notice that we hold tension in our backs when we feel overwhelmed or stressed. By recognizing this pattern, we can work to release the emotional stressors and retrain our body to respond differently to stress, ultimately leading to a reduction in pain. Self-awareness also allows us to connect with our intuition and inner wisdom. When we are in tune with our bodies and emotions, we can better understand our own needs and make conscious choices that support our healing process.

Here are some ways in which you can show up for yourself and get into the habit of nurturing self-awareness:

- **Get into the habit of regularly asking yourself, what is it that I need right now?** This is something that is so incredibly life-changing. I cannot even begin to stress how important it is. It's a generous act of self-love toward yourself. And a big, bold reminder that you matter too.
- **Get into the habit of asking yourself if a certain behavior or emotion is serving you in any way or form.** This is something that can help you become more intentional with your life and boost the levels of self-awareness that you have. It's a great starting point in identifying what needs to change and how as well as a divine opportunity for something else to morph into something beautiful.
- **Approach your emotions with less judgment and more curiosity.** Shift your perspective from the idea that they are something to be feared or suppressed, but rather as a source for valuable insight and information. Instead of labeling them as "good" or "bad," you might rather ask yourself questions like what triggered this emotion? What is it that they are trying to tell you? What's amiss? What particular experience or event is this emotion reminding me of? What can I do for myself to make myself feel better in this whole situation?
- **Let go of comparison and lean into gratitude.** You are not them, and they are not you. By allowing yourself to embrace your story and not shaming yourself into change, you learn to become more intentional in your own healing journey; you start doing things for yourself and not for other people, which is a more sustainable way to approach growth.
- **Create more than you consume.** In today's society, we are constantly bombarded with information and entertainment, from social media to streaming services, which is why it's all the easier to

dissociate. While there is nothing wrong with enjoying these things, it is important to remember that they are designed to be consumed, not created. To truly grow and develop as individuals, we must strive to create more than we consume. This could mean anything from writing a book to starting a business or simply volunteering in your community. By focusing on creation, we not only improve ourselves but also contribute to the world around us and make a positive impact on others. So, take a step back and ask yourself, are you consuming more than you create? If so, it may be time to reevaluate your priorities and start focusing on creating something meaningful.

- **Start focusing more on where most of your energy is going.**
- **Notice the little things that inspire you to be better.** This can be anything. From the little acts of kindness that you see other strangers doing for other people to any positive feedback that you receive or small victories that you get. By noticing these little things, you'll learn to develop a greater appreciation for all the good in your life, which can contribute to you leading a more fulfilling life.

I really love that expression: the only way out is through, more especially in the context of self-awareness. With tons of compassion and intentionality around what we find when we check in with ourselves, we can get through some of our toughest seasons and emotions.

2

Understanding the Body-Mind Connection

"Your body hears everything your mind says."

— NAOMI JUDD

If our bodies can't express it, our minds will repress. That mind-body connection is real. Deny one, and the other will follow. Take a moment to think about this: how often do you stop yourself from listening to your body's cues and messages?

Here's the thing: your mind is a treasure chest brimming with a dazzling array of thoughts, emotions, and experiences. Some of these treasures are iridescent and sparkle brightly, while others are hidden away in the depths, concealed from view. But what happens when the contents of this chest become too overwhelming for the mind to handle?

The mind becomes cluttered and clouded with negative thoughts and emotions that make it difficult to process information. Our bodies and minds are intricately connected, like two performers in a show. They

13

rely on each other to create a harmonious performance, to move in sync, each taking their turn in the spotlight. But every now and then, the show might take somewhat of a twisted turn. When that happens, a torrent of emotions might surge through your veins, threatening to burst forth like a mighty storm. Anxiety, anger, sadness—all demanding a stage to express themselves. Yet, sometimes, the body fails to find the words or actions to convey these emotions adequately.

That's when the mind steps in—the ultimate escape artist, I sometimes like to call it. It waves its wand and whispers, "Repress!" In a swift motion, and helps you sweep those overwhelming emotions and experiences into the shadows of the subconscious. It's a defense mechanism, a coping strategy to protect us from the turmoil that threatens to consume us. But here's the thing that we have to understand, just because the mind has tucked these emotions away doesn't mean they've disappeared. Oh no, they're lurking in the shadows, waiting for a chance to resurface; Like a pressure cooker left unattended, they build up steam, slowly but surely. And when that pressure becomes too much to bear, the mind's magic trick unravels.

Repression often manifests in various ways. It seeps into our dreams, where the subconscious tries to make sense of the buried emotions. It may manifest as physical symptoms—headaches, stomachaches, or fatigue—signaling the body's plea for attention. Or it may even manifest in unexpected outbursts when those repressed emotions burst forth like an untamed beast, catching us off guard in the most unexpected of ways.

When the body speaks, we ought to listen to what it wants and honor it's wrong. This is why:

The Body has Boundaries and Impulses That We Can Trust

The body is a complex yet remarkable thing. It has all of these mechanisms that allow us to engage and interact with the world around us. It possesses a pearl of innate wisdom and signals that can help guide us through life as we heal, evolve and grow. One of the foundational aspects of its existence is the boundaries that serve to help us differentiate what is and isn't for us. These are the instincts, feelings, and sensations that help us define our safe spaces, spaces that protect us from the world out there.

Trusting our bodies' boundaries and impulses is a non-negotiable aspect of our psychological well-being. It's what helps us recognize and identify our needs; it's what gives us the wisdom to honor our wiring and to take care of ourselves in healthy and sustainable ways. When we trust ourselves, our bodies, we become more in tune with our emotions, our physical sensations and our instincts. This knowledge that we acquire simply by being in tune is what helps us make decisions that align with our values, leading to a stronger sense of purpose and direction.

Some of the ways through which our bodies communicate boundaries with us might include:

They send messages through pain and discomfort. Pain is one of the most obvious ways our bodies communicate boundaries. When we experience pain or discomfort, it is often a signal that there is something that needs to be addressed. For instance, if we overexert ourselves during exercise, our body may send us pain signals to indicate that we need to stop or slow down to prevent injury.

15

Fatigue and rest. The body has a natural rhythm that includes the need for rest and rejuvenation. When we're tired, it is a clear indication that our bodies require rest. Ignoring this boundary can lead to exhaustion, decreased productivity, and potential health issues. Respecting our body's need for rest allows us to show up for our lives with vitality and an infectious kind of energy.

Hunger and fullness cues. The body has a built-in mechanism to regulate our food intake. When we feel hungry, it is a signal that our body needs nourishment and energy. On the other hand, when we feel full or satisfied, it is a boundary indicating that we have consumed enough food. Listening to these cues helps us maintain a healthy relationship with food and avoid overeating or undereating.

Our bodies also have boundaries when it comes to personal space and touch. We may feel uncomfortable or violated when someone invades our personal space without consent or touches us inappropriately. These bodily boundaries are important for maintaining our sense of safety, autonomy, and sense of self-respect.

Our bodies can also communicate boundaries related to our emotional and mental well-being. Feelings like overwhelm, stress, or anxiety can signal that we need to take a step back, practice self-care, or seek support. When we ignore these, we might find ourselves burnt out, in a state of emotional distress, and completely disassociated from our external worlds.

It is not our job to pretzel ourselves into something that we're not. Dimming or silencing our bodies' voices only creates an array of psychological health issues in the longer run. The mindset begins in the body. What we think comes directly from what we feel. How are you holding and honoring your body's boundaries right now? How can you create more open space for your body's sensations to exist as freely as they can?

The Body Stores Information

Have you ever come across a scent or taste that transports you back to a particular memory? It's as if your mind and body unite to recreate an experience from the past. This is all a testament to the remarkable ability of our bodies to store information.

Memories are not solely confined to the recesses of our minds. They are intricately intertwined with our physical sensations, etched into the fabric of our bodies. Our senses of smell, taste, touch, sight, and sound all contribute to the rich tapestry of memories that define us. When we encounter a specific scent or taste, it triggers a cascade of neural connections in our brain, reviving associated memories and emotions. This phenomenon, known as "sensory memory recall," highlights how our bodies serve as repositories of information.

Think about the distinctive aroma of freshly baked cookies wafting through the air. In an instant, you may find yourself transported back to your grandmother's kitchen, engulfed in a flood of nostalgia. The smell of the cookies becomes a portal, unlocking a trove of memories, conversations, and emotions stored within your body. In the same way, a particular taste can serve as a time machine, whisking you away to moments long gone. Perhaps the tang of a childhood treat, or the bitterness of a certain fruit can awaken forgotten experiences, allowing you to relive them with vivid clarity.

Our bodies possess an innate ability to absorb and retain information from the world around us. This is why physical sensations are so closely linked to our memories. The neural pathways connecting our senses to the brain form a complex network, capturing the nuances of our experiences and encoding them into our very being.

When we experience challenging or traumatic events, our bodies also often absorb and retain these experiences in various ways. The imprints of these experiences can manifest themselves in various ways, such as changes in the ways our brains function or the way we think, muscle tension, and sometimes even chronic pain. Recognizing and understanding how this interconnectedness works and how the body and mind are both affected, helps us gain insight into the root causes of our physical and emotional distress. Here are some of the remarkable ways through which ways this knowledge can support our healing journey:

It Helps in the Process of Identifying Our Triggers

Your mind is your home, a cozy space that feels like a snug blanket wrapped around you on a chilly day. This is the place where you can relax and unwind without fear or anxiety. I want you to think of this home as a representation of the overall state of your well-being. If you have some unresolved trauma from the past, that trauma can be like a storm passing through your house, leaving behind some broken windows and damaged walls.

Our triggers are the unexpected guests who come knocking on the door. These represent events, situations, or reminders that connect to past traumas and can unknowingly awaken the storm within us. When triggered, it's as if they accidentally bump into those broken windows and damaged walls, causing a cascade of emotions and reactions.

Let's say you had a very turbulent childhood growing up. The sound of voices rising or people shouting may be a trigger for you. When these triggers occur, it's like a guest knocking on your door and accidentally shattering one of the broken windows. Suddenly, a gust of wind rushes in, stirring up the emotions and memories associated with the accident. You might feel fear, anxiety or even experience vivid flashbacks.

Triggers can affect us in various ways. They can elicit intense emotional responses, such as anger, sadness, or panic. They might also lead to physical reactions like increased heart rate, sweating, or feeling lightheaded. Sometimes, they lead to dissociation or withdrawal from the present moment, and it's almost as if we're closing ourselves off in a separate room of the house in an attempt to protect ourselves from the storm.

In understanding these triggers that activate our body's stress or trauma response, we can become more aware of the situations, people, or environments that may be contributing to our distress. We can repair and rebuild our physical house after a storm; we can create a safe and resilient space within ourselves, ready to face whatever unexpected guests may come knocking on our door.

They Help Us Uncover Our Patterns of Behavior

Our patterns of behavior are cues inside of us that can help us understand what's going on inside of us. If you are someone who tends to overeat when stressed, for example, it could be an indication that you are the kind of person who uses food to cope with difficult emotions. Or on another note, if you are someone who tends to turn toward partners who are emotionally unavailable, it could be a sign that you fear intimacy. Understanding the messages that our bodies send to us can help us unpack how unhealthy or healthy these patterns of behaviors are, which will enable us to effectively start working on changing them.

Releasing stored trauma: Traumatic experiences can become trapped in our bodies, leading to emotional and physical distress. Techniques such as somatic experiencing, somatic therapy, eye movement desensitization and reprocessing (EMDR), or body-based therapies can help release these stored traumas, allowing for healing and resolution.

Enhance self-care practices: I like to think of self-care as gardening work. Just as a garden cannot thrive without proper care and maintenance, our souls and bodies cannot thrive without proper attention and care. When we recognize how the body stores information, we can prioritize self-care practices that support our healing journey. Engaging in activities like exercise, meditation, deep breathing, or bodywork can help release tension, promote relaxation, and cultivate a greater sense of well-being. These practices can also help us connect with our bodies and better understand our unique needs.

The Body Speaks Through Movements and Sensations

Imagine yourself standing on a beautiful sandy beach, feeling the warmth of the sun on your skin and the gentle breeze caressing your face. As you take a deep breath, you can almost taste the saltiness of the ocean in the air. At this very moment, your body is speaking to you, not with words, but through sensations and movement. Isn't that just incredible?

Our bodies are powerful communication vessels, constantly conveying messages through the art and language of sensations and movement.

Every twitch, shiver, or tingle is a secret code with a deeper meaning. It's as if our bodies are telling us a story, and if we pay close attention, we can become masters at deciphering its messages.

Sensations are the whispers of our body, its way of sharing its experiences with us. When you touch something hot, your body responds with sharp, instantaneous pain, urging you to remove your hand to protect yourself. Likewise, when you feel a gentle touch or a warm embrace, your body responds with a comforting sensation, igniting a feeling of connection and love.

But it's not just through pain and pleasure that our bodies communicate. Have you ever felt a knot in your stomach when you were anxious or had a tingling sensation down your spine when you felt excited? These physical manifestations are the body's way of expressing emotions that words alone may struggle to capture. Our bodies become the storyteller, painting a vivid picture of our inner world.

Movement, on the other hand, is the dance of our body, an expression of our desires, intentions, and emotions. Think of a ballet dancer gracefully gliding across the stage or a football player sprinting toward the goal. Their bodies speak volumes without uttering a single word. The fluidity, strength, and rhythm of their movements convey messages of passion, determination, and joy.

Just as sensations are intertwined with emotions, movement is inti-mately linked to our thoughts and intentions. Picture a person slumped in their chair, shoulders hunched, and head down. This posture reflects physical tiredness and a lack of confidence or enthusiasm. Imagine someone standing tall with an open chest, a genuine smile, and purposeful strides. Their body language radiates self-assurance, inviting others to engage and connect with them. Our bodies are the instruments through which we experience the world, and they speak a language that goes beyond words. By listening to the sensations and observing the movements of our bodies, we can gain valuable insights into our physical well-being, emotional states, and even our relationships with others.

An Exercise to Connect to the Sensations of Your Body

- Find a quiet space where you won't be interrupted for a few minutes.
- Sit or stand comfortably with your eyes closed and take a few deep breaths.
- Focus on your feet and try to feel the soles of your feet against the ground. Notice any sensations, such as warmth or coldness, tingling, or pressure.
- Move your attention up your body to your legs. Feel the weight of your legs against the surface supporting you. Notice any sensations like tension or relaxation.
- Now, bring your attention to your back. Notice any sensations in your spine, shoulders, and neck, such as tightness or ease.
- Next, focus on your chest and take a deep breath. Notice the sensation of your lungs filling up with air and the expansion of your chest.
- Move to your arms and hands. Do they feel heavy or light? Are they warm or cold?
- Finally, bring your attention to your head, neck, and face. Notice any sensations such as tension or relaxation in your facial muscles.
- Take a few more deep breaths, and when you're ready, open your eyes.

Challenge yourself: Pay attention next time you feel a shiver down your spine or a flutter in your stomach. Your body is trying to tell you something. Embrace the language of sensations and movement, and embark on a journey of self-discovery and connection with the world around you.

How Stress and Trauma Affect Your Body

Fight or flight mode is our body's natural response to stressful or traumatic events. This kind of response triggers a series of psychological changes in our bodies. It's what makes our hearts beat faster. Our breath quickens, and our muscles are all ready for action. It's literally the body's version of "all hands on deck." Being stuck in a fight or flight response mode can look like this:

- Becoming extremely reactive or defensive when you're being held accountable for something or criticized.
- Ignoring or shutting out other people's perspectives.
- Feeling easily threatened in some way or another.
- Shouting or becoming overly aggressive during conflict situations.
- An explosive temper with a tendency to experience shame afterward.
- Avoidance: physically leaving uncomfortable situations or abiding difficult topics or hard conversations.
- Escaping reality through distractions such as choosing to overwork yourself or other types of coping mechanisms.
- Struggling with commitment and feeling trapped.

When we're stuck in fight-or-flight mode, we're essentially running off on survival energy of cortisol, adrenaline, chaos, and fear. We're terrified that if we simply just let ourselves be for a moment or two, that if we slow down, we're never going to get back up and go again. We worry that if we don't overactivated our nervous systems with something-or anything that will give us some kind of rush, we will not be able to function effectively.

While fight or flight mode can be lifesaving in immediate danger situations, when we experience chronic stress, it can lead to a range of health problems ranging from anxiety, depression, health issues, and other heart-related diseases. These are all conditions that can negatively impact and affect our daily lives, making it more difficult to interact and engage fully with our lives. Chronic stress also influences our immune systems because of increased hormone production. When this happens, we also become more susceptible to illness.

It's important that we learn and teach ourselves how to manage stress, navigate life's challenges, and develop healthier coping mechanisms without relying too much on our flight or fight responses. When we allow ourselves to ease into the cycles of our bodies when we connect more deeply to them, our bodies can recover and tap into an energy that is much more powerful, grounding, and nourishing to our souls.

Releasing Tension With Body Awareness Tools

We can't fully embrace the gift of what it means to be human without being in our bodies. This is something that we need to remind ourselves of over and over again. Connecting with that body of yours is also about learning to listen because it always knows the way and always will.

When it comes to releasing tension and stress in the body, there are plenty of tools that we can use to regulate our nervous systems. Let's explore what some of them are:

Deep Breathing: Our breath is one of the most powerful tools that we have to regulate our emotional and mental states. By paying attention to the sensations of our breath, we gain greater awareness of the internal experience and learn to balance the body and the mind. Focus on inhaling deeply through your nose, allowing your abdomen to expand, and then exhaling slowly through your mouth. This technique can be practiced anywhere, at any time, in whatever space feels safest to you. Another effective way through which you can tap into the power of your breath is by using your inhales and exhales as anchors for attention. Focus on the sensations of air filling your lungs and leaving your body. By noticing these breaths, you can bring your attention back to the present moment and reduce the amount of stress and distractions around you.

In your more challenging situations, how about you take a few moments of pause before responding? By creating more space between your thoughts and actions, you empower yourself to make more intentional choices.

Breathing through your belly: Belly breathing, also called diaphragmatic breathing, is a powerful technique that involves taking deep breaths that expand your belly upon inhaling and contract it upon exhaling. This technique can help stimulate the vagus nerve and activate the parasympathetic nervous system, leading to relaxation and stress reduction.

Here's an exercise that I want you to try out:

The Magic of Diaphragmatic Breathing: A Stress-Relief Exercise
The human body is a complex system, entwining physical, emotional, and mental aspects into one interconnected web. Stress, an unwelcome

25

guest, can infiltrate this system and trigger an array of detrimental effects. However, our own bodies harbor a simple yet potent antidote—diaphragmatic breathing. This exercise, rooted in the power of the breath, is a gateway to stress relief and enhanced well-being.

Step 1: Set the stage

Dim the lights if you prefer, or light some aromatic candles for a calming ambiance. Comfort is key, so settle down in a position that feels good to you, whether it's sitting upright, lying down, or leaning against a supportive surface.

Step 2: Connect with your body

Close your eyes and take a moment to connect with your body. Feel the weight of your body against your support and the texture of your clothes against your skin. Notice your natural breathing pattern without trying to change it. This is your baseline, your starting point.

Step 3: Diaphragmatic breathing

Now, place one hand on your chest and the other on your belly. Inhale deeply through your nose, allowing your belly to rise as you fill your diaphragm—think of filling a balloon. Your chest should remain relatively still. Exhale slowly through your mouth, letting your belly fall. This is diaphragmatic breathing, also known as "belly breathing."

Step 4: Mindful Breathing

Continue this pattern: a deep inhale through your nose, belly rising, and a slow exhale through your mouth, belly falling. As you breathe, become an observer of your experience. Notice the sensation of air entering and leaving your body. Feel the rhythmic rise and fall of your belly. If your mind wanders, gently guide it back to your breath.

Step 5: Body scan

As you settle into this breathing rhythm, start a mental scan from the top of your head to the tips of your toes. With each exhale, imagine releasing tension from each part of your body. Relax your forehead, loosen your jaw, drop your shoulders, unclench your hands, and so on. You might imagine stress draining away from you like water down a stream.

Step 6: Return and reflect

After about 10 to 15 minutes—or whenever you feel ready—bring your attention back to the room. Wiggle your fingers and toes, and slowly open your eyes. Take a moment to reflect on any changes in your physical or emotional state.

Diaphragmatic breathing is more than a stress relief tool. It's a journey into the body, an exploration of the breath's power, and an opportunity to cultivate mindfulness. It is a testament to our body's inherent ability to heal and find balance. As you practice this exercise, remember that it's a process, not a destination. Every breath is a step toward greater well-being and stress-free living. Happy breathing!

Progressive Muscle Relaxation (PMR): PMR involves systematically tensing and then relaxing different muscle groups in your body. By consciously tensing and releasing each muscle group, you can identify areas of tension and encourage them to relax. Start from your toes and work your way up, focusing on one muscle group at a time. This practice promotes deep relaxation and helps release overall bodily tension.

Mindfulness Meditation: Mindfulness meditation cultivates present-moment awareness and non-judgmental acceptance of bodily sensations. By bringing your attention to the sensations in your body, you can become more attuned to areas of tension. With practice, you can learn to observe tension without judgment and allow it to release naturally. Mindfulness meditation can be done through guided practices, apps, or attending meditation classes.

Here's an example of a mindfulness meditation that you can try to cultivate that present moment awareness:

- Begin by finding a comfortable space to sit or lie down and allowing your body to settle into a calm and relaxed state. Take a deep breath in, and as you exhale, let go of any tension or stress that you may be holding onto.
- Now, bring your attention to the present moment. Notice any sensations in your body, such as the feeling of your breath moving in and out of your body, the weight of your body against the surface you're sitting or lying on, or any areas of tension.
- As you focus on your breath, imagine yourself breathing in fresh, clean air and exhaling any negative thoughts or emotions. You may find it helpful to visualize these thoughts as a cloud or mist, which dissipates as you breathe out.
- Allow yourself to fully immerse in the sensations of your body and the present moment without judgment or distraction. If your mind begins to wander, gently bring your attention back to your breath and the present moment.
- Take a few more deep breaths, and when you're ready, slowly open your eyes and take a moment to reorient yourself to the world around you.

Stretching and Yoga: Physical movement, such as stretching and yoga, is excellent for releasing tension in the body. Engaging in gentle stretches and yoga poses helps increase flexibility, improve blood circulation, and relieve muscle tension. Pay attention to areas of tightness, and focus on gentle stretching exercises that target those specific muscles or areas. Regular practice can lead to increased body awareness and overall relaxation.

Body Scanning: Body scanning is a technique that involves systematically directing your attention to different parts of your body, observing sensations, and releasing tension. Start from the top of your head and slowly move down, paying attention to each body part. As you scan, notice any areas of tension or discomfort. Imagine sending your breath to those areas and visualizing the tension melting away. I have, for example, noticed that one of the areas where I hold most of my anxiety symptoms is in my muscles. The main points are my jaw, the sides of my neck, and my shoulders. If these are areas in which you also struggle, here is a mindful body scanning technique that you can try out.

- Start off by unclenching your jaw.
- Lower your shoulders.
- Release and try to let go of the "gripping' in your stomach.
- Stretch your legs.
- Lift your toes and see if you can get them to relax.
- Unclench your fists.
- Check your posture.
- Roll your neck around in circles.
- And then try to relax your forehead.

It's a rhythm of softening, releasing, breathing again, and reminding yourself that you are not drowning. You are here, practicing presence, and will breathe again.

Each of our experiences of tension and the most effective tools for release may vary. It's important to listen to your body and find the techniques that work best for you. Regular practice and patience are key to developing body awareness and effectively releasing tension.

Things I Want You To Remember:

- Connecting to your body is a process, and it's okay to start small. Be patient and celebrate each step forward, no matter how small or insignificant it may seem.
- Pay attention to the signals your body sends you. Whether it's hunger, fatigue, or stress, your body communicates its needs through various sensations. Learn to interpret these signals and respond accordingly.
- Mindfulness is a gateway to presence and connection. Engage in activities that promote mindfulness, such as yoga, meditation, or deep breathing exercises. These practices can help you become more aware of your body and its sensations, fostering a deeper connection.
- Engage your senses to connect with your body. Take a moment to appreciate the taste, smell, texture, and sounds around you. By fully immersing yourself in the present moment, you become more attuned to your body's responses.
- Nourish Your Body. The body rewards us when we reward it. The nourishment of your body goes beyond just food. Pay attention to the quality and quantity of the food you consume and the level of hydration, sleep, and exercise you engage in. Prioritize self-care to foster a stronger mind-body connection. Move with Intention: Engage in physical activities that bring you joy and allow you to connect with your body. Whether it's dancing, hiking, or practicing a sport, find activities that make you feel alive and present in your

body.

- Let go of any judgment or criticism toward your body. Accept it as it is, knowing that it's unique and capable of amazing things. Embrace your body's strengths and appreciate all that it allows you to do.
- Find creative outlets to express yourself and connect with your body. Whether it's through art, dance, or writing, allow your body to be a vessel for self-expression and self-discovery.
- Take time to explore your body and its capabilities. Engage in activities that promote body awareness, such as stretching, massage, or even simply taking a few moments to check in with yourself throughout the day.
- As you continue to learn and develop a stronger connection with your body, celebrate every milestone and achievement. Recognize the growth you've made and use it as fuel to continue deepening your connection.

In the next chapter, we unpack self-exploration and healing, what it means to be us, and to make our own breakthrough in the healing process. Are you ready? I know I am!

3

Techniques for Self-Exploration and Healing

"Knowing who you are on a deep and intimate level is how you protect yourself from internalizing disempowering opinions about yourself."

— CHER HAMPTON

Most of who we think we are is constructed to cope with life while growing up. Evaluating the traits and personalities that we have will help us identify whether or not they're from our authentic selves or from our coping, surviving, or conditioned selves.

Self-exploration is introspection and self-discovery. It involves delving into our thoughts, emotions, beliefs, values, and experiences in order to gain a deeper understanding of ourselves. It is how we unearth our authentic selves and how we separate from societal expectations, conditioning, and external influences. It is a delicate process of peeling back layers, examining our motivations, desires, and fears, and weaving a genuine connection with ourselves.

Self-exploration and healing are deeply intertwined. When we experience challenges or trauma, we often lose sight of who we truly are. We adopt coping or defense mechanisms and put on masks to protect ourselves from pain or to meet societal expectations. These adaptations often lead to a disconnection from our core essence, leading to emotional distress, inner conflict, and a sense of dissatisfaction.

In choosing to embark on a journey of self-exploration, we open ourselves up to the possibility of healing. It allows us to confront and process past wounds, traumas, and unresolved emotions. Through self-reflection, we gain clarity about their triggers, patterns of behavior, and the limiting beliefs that may be holding us back from living a fulfilling life.

Self-exploration also facilitates personal growth and transformation. It is an agent of empowerment that prompts us to identify our passions, strengths, and values, enabling us to make choices aligned with our core beings. We develop a greater sense of self-acceptance, self-compassion, and self-love. This, in turn, fosters emotional well-being, resilience, and a stronger sense of identity. Let's not forget how it enriches our interpersonal relationships. By understanding ourselves better, we can communicate our needs, desires, and boundaries more effectively. It allows for deeper connections with others based on authenticity, empathy, and vulnerability.

Doing the messy and hard work related to self-exploration was the best thing that I have done for myself. It's really what led to an important realization about my life and priorities. It was one ordinary afternoon, and I just got so lost. I was doing well in my studies, and my career

33

prospects looked promising. I had a steady and comfortable life, but I couldn't help but feel that there was something still missing.

Initially, I was reluctant to confront my own inner turmoil. Why? Well, there are several reasons for that:

- Firstly, it was a fear of the unknown. The process of self-exploration often leads to us discovering things or truths that we are not yet ready to acknowledge. I know that this fear is what made me a little more reluctant to dig deeper into my heart and my mind.
- There was also the fear of change holding me back. Self-exploration makes us realize that there are things that we need to change in our lives and in our lives if we, in any way or form, are looking to heal. The fear and anxiety related to this are often what leads to resistance toward the process.
- Our egos are also essentially the voices within us that affirm our sense of self and identity. They're what make us feel safe and secure in our identities. They're what establish a sense of comfort in our lives—even if that comfort is destructive and hinders our progress.
- Our long-held beliefs and expectations too are actors that we cannot ignore.. Most of us have long-held assumptions about ourselves. That's what limits us from doing that necessary self-work, what makes it difficult for us to see ourselves beyond what is true about ourselves and our place in the world.

"Was I going to disrupt the comfort that I had worked so hard to build?" That is the one recurrent thought that I just couldn't seem to shake, but eventually, I realized that ignoring all that I was feeling would only result in things getting a lot worse for me. So, I dug—I dug deep into all my traumas and current fears. Was it easy? Definitely not. But it

was so utterly and entirely worth it. I unearthed a world of buried emotions, beliefs, and patterns. This messy work was all along, the key to unlocking a more fulfilling life for myself.

I know without a doubt that you, too, can do the necessary self-exploratory work. It won't be easy, but I know that you have it within you—you possess that inner strength, and over the next couple of pages, we're going to spend some time unpacking how you can do that.

Techniques for Self-Exploration

Embarking on a journey of self-exploration is an exhilarating and transformative process. It's a voyage that takes us deep within ourselves, unraveling the layers of thought, emotions, and experiences. Through various techniques, we can embark on this adventure, peering into the depths of our being and uncovering hidden treasures. From journaling and meditation to creative expression and seeking feedback, these techniques offer a compass to navigate the vast landscape of your inner world. So, grab your metaphorical backpack, and let's delve into the techniques that will unlock the doors to self-understanding and personal growth.

Therapies for Self-Soothing

Self-soothing describes our ability to regulate our emotional states. It's all about observing our behaviors and asking ourselves what behaviors we can apply in that current moment to make ourselves feel better. It's the equivalent of saying: "Hi there, I am here for you. How can I help myself in times of great there."

Traumas are like big storms that shake us from the steady foundations we've built our lives upon. They can be scary experiences that leave us feeling hurt, frightened, and overwhelmed. And just like a storm can damage a house, traumas can affect our ability to self-soothe.

Self-soothing is like giving ourselves a warm hug when feeling down. But when we've experienced past traumas, it can be harder to find those soothing tools. The storm of trauma may have jumbled them up, making it difficult to know what helps us feel safe and comforted.

That's why it's important to learn to self-soothe again. It's like untangling a knot in a string. By gently exploring our feelings and understanding how our traumas have affected us, we can start to put ourselves back together.

Learning to self-soothe doesn't mean forgetting about the past or pretending everything is okay. It is about finding healthy ways to comfort ourselves and regain a sense of control. It's like adding new tools to our toolbox, ones that help us feel safe, loved, and grounded.

When we can self-soothe, it's like having a superpower that helps us navigate life's challenges. We become more resilient and better equipped to handle stress and difficult emotions. It's like having a secret weapon against the storms that come our way.

Here are examples of some ways that you can self-soothe when you're feeling anxious:

Connect to your body. Lay on the ground and stretch as much as you can to shift your focus away from your thoughts and into your body. Figure out what activities your body enjoys and responds well to. These are all activities that will help you feel grounded when anxiety surfaces.

Use the environment around you. Our external environment can be such a powerful grounding technique. I mean, imagine yourself surrounded by nature, a gentle breeze caressing your face, and the melodic chirping of birds filling the air. How do you feel? Instantly, it's like a sense of calm washes over you, melting away stress and worries. That's the magic of the environment around us.

Our world is a symphony of sights, sounds, and sensations, each with the power to soothe our weary souls. Nature, in particular, has an incredible ability to heal and rejuvenate us. The vibrant colors of blooming flowers, the rhythmic crashing of ocean waves, and the rustling leaves of trees—these sights and sounds tap into our primal connection with the earth, reminding us of our place in the grand tapestry of life.

When we immerse ourselves in nature, our bodies respond in remarkable ways. The fresh scent of pine trees, the taste of clean air, and the warmth of sunlight on our skin trigger the release of endorphins, those delightful chemicals that make us feel good. Our heart rate lowers, blood pressure stabilizes, and stress hormones decrease. It's like nature has a secret recipe for tranquility.

But the environment isn't limited to sprawling landscapes; it extends to our immediate surroundings too. Creating a cozy sanctuary at home can work wonders for our well-being. Soft lighting, soothing colors, and comforting textures can transform a space into a sanctuary, providing a respite from the chaos of the world.

So, whether you choose to find solace in a natural setting or in the embrace of a cozy nook, remember that your space can be a powerful self-soothing technique. It has the extraordinary ability to transport you to a place of peace, restoring your balance and reconnecting us with your inner self.

Focus on pleasant memories or things that bring you sheer joy. Can I tell you something? This one is an absolute firm favorite of mine. When anxiety has too big a hold on me, I close my eyes and think of something that once made me smile or something that I am looking forward to. Sometimes it's the weekend or an upcoming trip with some friends. Painting these pictures often conjures up feelings of excitement inside that can regulate the anxiety that's bubbling within.

Touch Therapy for Self-Compassion

If you were walking out in public and took a hard fall while walking, what would you do? If you're like most people, you might feel embarrassed and start scolding yourself: "How could I be so clumsy? I'm such a failure!" But what if I told you there's a kinder, more supportive way to respond? That's where self-compassion comes in.

Self-compassion is the equivalent of having a personal cheerleader who's always by your side, ready to offer comfort and understanding when you're struggling or feeling down. It's all about treating yourself with the same kindness and compassion you would offer to a dear friend. Instead of beating yourself up for your mistakes, self-compassion invites you to embrace your humanity. It recognizes that everyone makes blunders, feels pain, and faces challenges. It's a reminder that you're not alone in your struggles.

Self-compassion involves three key elements: self-kindness, common humanity, and mindfulness. Firstly, self-kindness means being gentle and understanding with yourself when things go wrong. It's about offering words of encouragement instead of harsh criticism.

Common humanity reminds us that we are not alone in our experiences. It recognizes that everyone faces hardships and imperfections. So instead of feeling isolated, self-compassion helps us connect with others through a shared sense of humanity.

Finally, mindfulness plays a crucial role in self-compassion. It involves being present in the moment and acknowledging your emotions without judgment. By practicing mindfulness, you can observe your thoughts and feelings with curiosity and acceptance, fostering a compassionate attitude toward yourself.

Self-compassion is not about making excuses or avoiding personal growth. It's about creating a supportive and nurturing relationship with yourself. When you embrace self-compassion, you become more resilient, better equipped to handle challenges, and able to bounce back from setbacks.

Touch therapy and self-compassion go hand in hand. Touch therapy involves using techniques like self-massage, aromatherapy, acupressure, or energy healing to connect with your body and nurture your well-being. It's like a loving language that your body understands and responds to with gratitude.

When we practice touch therapy, we are essentially saying to ourselves, "Hey, body, I value and care for you." It's an act of radical self-acceptance and kindness. By intentionally touching ourselves with gentleness and love, we create a safe space where self-compassion can flourish.

39

Think about it–when you receive a comforting touch, like a hug or a gentle pat on the back, it immediately triggers a sense of comfort and reassurance. The same goes for touch therapy! When we engage in these practices, our bodies respond by releasing tension, reducing stress, and promoting relaxation.

Touch therapy can help us build a deeper connection with ourselves. It encourages us to listen to our bodies, understand our needs, and respond with nurturing touch. It's like having a heart-to-heart conversation with yourself through touch – a conversation that says, "You are worthy of love and care." Here are some examples of effective touch therapy methods that you can use.

Self-Massage: Self-massage is a wonderful way to show yourself some love and care through touch. It involves using your hands or tools like foam rollers or massage balls to apply gentle pressure on different parts of your body. Start by finding a quiet and comfortable space, and slowly work your way from head to toe, focusing on areas that hold tension or stress. As you massage, bring awareness to your body, and let the soothing touch promote relaxation and self-compassion.

Aromatherapy: Aromatherapy combines the power of touch with the therapeutic properties of essential oils. By using specific oils known for their calming, uplifting, or grounding effects, you can enhance your self-compassion practice. Dilute the essential oil of your choice with a carrier oil, like coconut or jojoba oil, and gently massage it onto your wrists, temples, or the soles of your feet. As you inhale the aroma, allow yourself to connect with the present moment and embrace self-compassion.

Acupressure: An ancient healing technique that involves applying pressure to specific points on the body to promote relaxation and balance. By gently pressing these points with your fingers or using a massage tool, you can stimulate the body's natural healing response. Find acupressure points like the "Third Eye" (between your eyebrows) or the "Inner Gate" (on your wrist) and apply gentle pressure for a few seconds. As you do this, take deep breaths, tune in to your body's sensations, and cultivate a sense of self-compassion.

Energy Healing: Energy healing, such as Reiki or Healing Touch, involves channeling healing energy into the body through touch or proximity. While it's often done by practitioners, you can also practice self-energy healing. Start by placing your hands on different parts of your body, focusing on areas that feel tense or imbalanced. Close your eyes, take deep breaths, and imagine warm, loving energy flowing through your hands and into your body. Allow this healing touch to nurture your self-compassion and promote a sense of well-being.

Grounding Techniques

Being grounded is the equivalent of having a steady anchor amidst the chaos of life. It feels centered, calm, and in control, even when you are faced with challenges or stress. Like a tree with deep roots, you are firmly planted and able to weather any storm that comes your way.

Being in a state of groundedness is having an awareness of our bodies and our emotions without judgment or attachment. A solid foundation that allows us to navigate life's ups and downs with a sense of inner peace and resilience. It is not about escaping reality or denying yourself of the difficult emotions that you're experiencing. It's about embracing them with acceptance and finding a sense of stability within yourself. It acknowledges and processes your emotions but not allowing them to consume or overwhelm you.

Grounding techniques can be incredibly helpful in helping to alleviate some anxiety, dissociation, or trauma symptoms. Let's explore some of those techniques that you can try.

Mental Grounding

Mental grounding techniques are tools that can help us stay present, focused, and connected to reality when we're feeling overwhelmed, anxious, or disconnected. They are the anchors that bring us back to the here and now, allowing us to regain a sense of stability and calm.

Imagine yourself caught in a whirlwind of thoughts and emotions, and it feels like your mind is taking you on a wild roller coaster ride. Mental grounding techniques serve as the safety harness that keeps you securely grounded in the present moment, preventing you from getting swept away by the chaos.

One popular mental grounding technique is called "5-4-3-2-1." It goes like this:

- Look around and find five things you can see. It could be objects in the room, colors, or anything in your surroundings. Really take the time to notice the details of each item, their shape, texture, or movement.
- Now, shift your focus and identify four things you can feel physically. It could be the sensation of your clothes against your skin, the texture of the ground beneath your feet, or the warmth of a mug in your hands. Pay attention to the different qualities of touch and how they make you feel.

- Next, listen for three things you can hear. It could be the sound of traffic outside, birds chirping, or the hum of a refrigerator. Tune in to the layers of sound around you, both near and distant, and let them anchor you to the present moment.
- Notice two things you can smell. It could be the scent of fresh coffee, a flower, or even something subtle like the aroma of a familiar place. Take a deep breath and allow the smells to ground you in the present.
- Finally, you focus on one thing you can taste. It could be a sip of water, a piece of fruit, or the lingering flavor of a meal. Pay attention to the taste, temperature, and texture, savoring the sensations it provides.

By engaging your senses in this way, you're redirecting your attention away from racing thoughts and worries and bringing it back to the physical world. These grounding techniques can be done quickly, discreetly, and almost anywhere, allowing you to find a sense of stability and calmness amidst the chaos.

Here are a couple of other examples and exercises that you can try:

- **Play a memory game**: Look at a detailed picture for five to 10 seconds and then flip those over or turn away and recall as many of those details as you can remember.
- **Categories**: Choose a broad category (e.g.) that could be cars, singers, or whatever tickles your fancy, and see how many items in that you can list in about a minute.
- **Use math and numbers**: count backward by hundreds, count in threes or go through specific times tables.
- **Recite something**. That can be a poem, a song, or a monologue from a favorite show. You can choose whether you will do this out

loud or in your head.

- **Find and cling to an anchoring phrase**. This can be a phrase that describes who you are, where you are, and what you are doing. What's the time? What's the date
- **Visualize an enjoyable or satisfying task**. Picture yourself doing this task, walk through it step by step, and imagine how it would feel to do this task.
- **Try to describe what is around you**. Spend a couple of minutes lapping up your surroundings. And notice what you are seeing. Engage all five of your senses and try to provide as much detail as you can.

Also, note that these are general exercises. They may or may not work, depending on your unique situation or preferences. For example, if math or numbers get you really stressed out, then doing a math-based exercise may be more stressful than it is grounding, so try and find something that works for you and leave out what does not work.

Emotional Grounding

Emotional grounding is a practice that helps us regulate our emotions and maintain a sense of stability and balance during times of emotional distress or overwhelm.

The whole concept is rooted in the understanding that our emotions can sometimes be intense and overwhelming, and we may experience difficulty in managing or processing them effectively. Emotional grounding techniques aim to tie us to the present moment, redirect our focus away from distressing thoughts or emotions, and promote a sense of calm and stability.

Using affirmations or encouraging statements to challenge negative or distressing thoughts is one of the most effective ways to promote a more positive and balanced mindset. But it's not always as simple as reciting a positive mantra or speaking the anxiety and trauma away. If we have made a habit out of talking negatively, it can be challenging to shift the mindset and start believing in the power of positive affirmations.

It takes a lot of time and repetition to create new patterns in our thinking. Also, sometimes, we're resistant to change or have limiting beliefs that prevent us from accepting the validity of our positive affirmations. To make sure that our positive affirmations are actually working for us, we have to focus more on consistency. The key to making them work and actually believing them is repeating them consistently. This is what can help us create new patterns in our thinking and shift our mindsets toward more positivity.

Belief, too, is an important element of the equation. We have to believe in the affirmation that we are saying for it to actually work. Our minds are wired to focus on what we believe to be true, so we have to make sure that we use affirmations and statements that resonate with us, statements that feel true and believable.

Match your words with action. You can't just recite an affirmation and magically expect all to be well and fixed. So, instead of just repeating your affirmations, why not try to take small steps to work on those goals that you are affirming. Doing that reinforces the belief that positive change is actually something that is doable and achievable.

1. *I am worthy of love and happiness.*
2. *I am allowed to prioritize my own well-being.*
3. *I am capable of overcoming any challenges that come my way.*

4. *I trust in my ability to make decisions that are right for me.*
5. *I am enough, just as I am at this moment.*
6. *I release any negative thoughts or emotions that no longer serve me.*
7. *I am deserving of all the good things that come into my life.*
8. *I choose to let go of past hurts and embrace forgiveness.*
9. *I am grateful for the lessons I have learned and the growth I have experienced.*
10. *I am surrounded by love and support from those who care about me.*
11. *I am allowed to take breaks and prioritize self-care.*
12. *I trust in the timing of my life and know that everything will work out for the best.*
13. *I am resilient and capable of bouncing back from any setbacks.*
14. *I am proud of myself for how far I have come on my journey.*
15. *I choose to focus on the present moment and find joy in the little things.*
16. *I am deserving of success and fulfillment in all areas of my life.*
17. *I trust in the process of life and surrender to the flow of the universe.*
18. *I am allowed to set boundaries and prioritize my own needs.*
19. *I am grateful for the love and support that surrounds me.*
20. *I am in control of my own happiness and choose to embrace positivity in my life.*

Physical Grounding

Physical grounding, as the name suggests, refers to a way of learning to reconnect with the present moment and our physical bodies. Techniques that are often used include mindfulness practices, therapy, or whenever someone feels overwhelmed, anxious, or disconnected from reality.

If you were standing atop a windy mountaintop and suddenly felt a bit unsteady or disoriented. What would you do? You would instinctively plant your feet firmly on the ground, feel the solid earth beneath you, and take a deep breath to regain your balance. That's an exact example of what physical grounding is!

Let's take a look at some of the small ways in which you can practice:

Grounding Objects: Carry a small object in your pocket, like a smooth stone, a keychain, or a piece of fabric. Whenever you feel disconnected or overwhelmed, hold the object in your hand, feel its texture, and focus on its weight. This tactile experience can anchor your attention and provide a sense of stability.

Stomp and Shake: Stand up and stomp your feet on the ground as if you're trying to shake off any tension or negative energy. You can also gently shake your hands or whole body to release tension and promote a sense of grounding. Physical grounding techniques are highly individual, so feel free to explore different techniques and find what works best for you. You can do this anytime, anywhere, and as often as needed to bring you back to the present moment and provide a sense of stability and calm. A few other techniques that sometimes get overlooked include:

- Running cool or warm water all over your hands
- Standing with your bare feet on the ground
- Holding on as tightly to your chair as you can
- Touching various objects around you
- Clenching and releasing your fists
- Digging your heels into the floor
- Eating something that is bursting with an infusion of flavor

Every time I feel that pain of past experiences coming up, I remind myself that pain is just a feeling. It's not who I am or something that gets to entirely define who I am. When we get caught up in all our pain, it's so easy to feel as if it's all there is that exists, but really, it's just one part of our experiences; the other parts are hiding and can be found when we ground ourselves.

Spiritual Grounding

Spiritual grounding is a practice that helps us establish a solid connection with our inner selves and the world around us. It is an essential aspect of spiritual well-being and can be seen as a way to anchor oneself in a stable and balanced state of mind.

Being spiritually grounded is often overlooked but is a vital aspect of the emotional healing process. This is what allows us to connect with a higher power or a deeper sense of purpose beyond ourselves. It involves nurturing our inner self and finding solace in something greater than our immediate circumstances. This spiritual grounding provides a sense of stability, strength, and clarity that can aid in our emotional healing journey.

When we are emotionally wounded, we often feel lost, confused, and overwhelmed. Our thoughts may spiral, and our emotions may fluctuate erratically. In such moments, spiritual grounding can serve as an anchor, helping us find stability amidst the chaos. By connecting with our spiritual essence, we tap into a wellspring of wisdom, resilience, and inner peace that can guide us toward healing.

Spirituality is not limited to religious beliefs; it encompasses a broader notion of connecting with our inner selves, others, nature, or a higher power. It allows us to transcend the limitations of our individualistic perspective and opens us up to a more expansive understanding of life. This broader perspective is a comforting reminder to us that our pain is not all-encompassing and that there is a greater purpose to our existence.

When we are spiritually grounded, we become more attuned to our inner voice, intuition, and higher consciousness. This heightened awareness enables us to identify and process our emotions more effectively. We learn to observe our thoughts and feelings without judgment, allowing them to flow through us rather than becoming entangled in them. This detachment empowers us to make healthier choices and respond to challenging situations with greater clarity and compassion.

I personally love the fact that spiritual grounding encourages us to cultivate gratitude, compassion, forgiveness, and acceptance. These qualities are essential in the emotional healing process because they encourage us to release resentment, anger, and negative emotions that hinder our progress. In choosing to lean more toward gratitude, we shift our focus from what is lacking to what we already have, fostering a positive mindset that supports our emotional well-being.

The techniques often vary and can be adapted to suit individual preferences and beliefs. Here are some commonly used techniques:

Spending time in nature can be a powerful way to nurture our spiritual well-being. Whether it's taking a walk in the park, hiking in the mountains, or simply sitting by a body of water, immersing ourselves in nature can provide a sense of peace and connection. It allows us to tap into the beauty and vastness of the natural world, reminding us of our place in the grand scheme of things and providing solace during the healing process.

Cultivating Gratitude: Practicing gratitude involves consciously acknowledging and appreciating the positive aspects of our lives. It shifts our focus from what is lacking to what we already have, fostering a sense of contentment and abundance. By regularly expressing gratitude for even the smallest blessings, we cultivate a positive mindset that supports emotional healing and spiritual growth.

- *Gratitude Journal*: Maintaining a daily or weekly gratitude journal can be a powerful practice. This could be as simple as jotting down one thing you're grateful for each day. Over time, this practice can help shift your mindset to focus more on the positive aspects of life.
- *Mindful Meditation*: Introducing gratitude during meditation can help incorporate it into your consciousness. You can do this by focusing your thoughts on something you're grateful for during your meditation practice.
- *Gratitude Letters*: Writing letters of gratitude to people who have had a positive impact on your life can be incredibly rewarding. You could send these letters or simply write them for your own reflection.
- *Gratitude Reminders*: Set up visual reminders around your home or workspace. These could be quotes, images, or anything that prompts you to feel grateful.
- *Gratitude Jar*: Keep a jar where you note down things for which you're grateful. When you're feeling low, you can pull out a note to remind yourself of the good in your life.
- *Acts of Kindness*: Performing small acts of kindness can foster a sense of gratitude in yourself and others. This could include helping a neighbor, volunteering, or simply offering a compliment to a

stranger.

- *Gratitude During Meals*: Before you eat, take a moment to appreciate the labor and resources that went into your meal. This can be a simple and regular practice of gratitude.
- *Gratitude Walks*: Take a walk specifically to appreciate your surroundings. Notice the beauty in nature, the architecture, the sounds—whatever speaks to you.
- *Gratitude in Conversations:* Try to incorporate more expressions of gratitude in your daily conversations. This can be as simple as expressing appreciation for a friend's support or acknowledging the effort someone put into their work.
- *Reflect on Challenges*: It might seem counter intuitive, but reflecting on challenges or difficult times and acknowledging the growth or strength that came from them can also cultivate gratitude.

Gratitude should never be about ignoring or glossing over difficulties but about recognizing and appreciating the good in our lives, even amidst challenges. It's a powerful tool for enhancing our overall happiness and well-being.

Creative activities like writing, painting, dancing, or playing an instrument can be a powerful way to nurture our spiritual well-being. These activities allow us to tap into our inner creativity, express ourselves authentically, and connect with something beyond our immediate circumstances. Creative expression can serve as a cathartic outlet for our emotions and contribute to our overall healing process.

Engaging in acts of kindness, volunteering, or simply being present for a loved one in need can help us develop a sense of interconnectedness and deepen our spiritual connection. By extending compassion to ourselves and others, we create a nurturing environment for emotional healing and spiritual growth.

Yoga: Yoga is not only a physical practice but also a spiritual one that can help us achieve a sense of grounding and connection with our inner selves. Let me go on a journey to explore how yoga can be used for spiritual grounding:

Imagine yourself standing tall, feet firmly planted on the ground, like the mighty oak tree. In yoga, this standing posture is called Tadasana or Mountain Pose. As you breathe in deeply, feel the energy of the Earth rising up through your feet and into your body. Visualize roots growing from the soles of your feet, anchoring you to the ground.

Now, let's transition into a beautiful and flowing sequence called the Sun Salutation. As you effortlessly move through the poses, keep your focus on the present moment, letting go of any worries or distractions. This flowing practice cultivates a sense of inner harmony and a connection between your body, mind, and spirit.

Next, we arrive at the heart of our yoga practice—the asanas, or yoga poses. As you move into different poses, pay attention to the physical sensations and the subtle energies they awaken within you. Each pose has its unique symbolism and can evoke different emotions and qualities.

For spiritual grounding, some poses can be particularly beneficial. For example, Balasana, or Child's Pose, encourages surrender and introspection. In this gentle pose, you can rest your forehead on the mat, symbolizing a humble connection with the Earth and an invitation to let go of any burdens.

Another spiritually grounding pose is Vrksasana or Tree Pose. Like a tree swaying in the wind, find your balance while standing on one leg, with the other leg lifted and the foot pressed against the inner thigh or calf. Imagine your body as the trunk of the tree and your arms as branches stretching toward the sky. Feel your roots growing deep into the ground, providing stability and strength.

Throughout your yoga practice, remember to bring awareness to your breath. Slow, deep breathing helps to calm the mind, relax the body, and create space for spiritual insights and connection. As you inhale, imagine you are breathing in fresh energy and inspiration, and as you exhale, release any tension or negativity.

Lastly, conclude your practice with Savasana, or Corpse Pose. Lie down on your back, close your eyes, and surrender to complete relaxation. This final pose allows for the integration and assimilation of the grounding energy and insights gained during your yoga practice.

A note to consider yoga is a personal and intimate journey. Feel free to explore different poses and sequences that resonate with you on a spiritual level. Let your practice be a creative expression of your own unique path toward spiritual grounding.

Remember, nurturing our spiritual well-being is something that is deeply personal. It's essential to explore different practices and find what resonates with us individually. Find and focus on the things that are meaningful to you. Don't just jump into things because someone said that it's something that you need to do. It's your story and your journey and therefore is something that should honor you.

Pendulation and Titration Techniques

Pendulation and titration are two techniques that focus on the sensory experiences that help in our recovery from trauma. Pendulation is the natural occurrence that takes place when our nervous systems are both exposed to stress and relaxation. Traumatic experiences often leave our nervous systems stuck in a heightened state which causes anxiety and hypervigilance. Pendulation techniques are used to help our nervous systems shift between states of activation and relaxation. Think of it like the rhythm of the ocean's waves. Just as they move back and forth between the sea and shore, our nervous systems sometimes move in between states of stress and relaxation. When the waves become too big, they can get all-consuming or too big.

One such example of this would be through the act of "tracking." This involves guiding your attention to different sensations, such as firmly planting your feet to the ground or allowing yourself to feel your breath moving in and outside you intensely. As you focus more of your attention on these sensations, your nervous system slowly begins to activate a more relaxed state for you.

Here's a step-by-step exercise that you can practically apply:

- Find a quiet, comfortable place to sit or lie down where you won't be disturbed.
- Begin by bringing your attention to your breath. Take a few deep, diaphragmatic breaths, focusing your attention on the sensation of the breath moving in and out of your body.
- Next, shift your attention to your feet. Feel the sensation of your feet pressing into the ground. Take a few moments to really focus on this sensation.

- Move your attention to your hands. Notice the feeling of your hands resting in your lap or against a surface if you're lying down. Focus on this sensation for a few moments.
- Return your attention to your breath, focusing on the sensation of the air moving in and out of your body. Take a few more deep breaths.
- Once again, bring your attention to your feet. Imagine that you're sending a soft, gentle wave of relaxation down your body and into your feet.
- Move your attention up your body, imagining this wave of relaxation spreading to your legs, hips, torso, arms, and head.
- As you move your attention through your body, allow yourself to let go of any tension or discomfort you may be holding. Imagine that you're releasing these sensations with each exhale.
- Finally, bring your attention back to your breath. Take a few more deep, diaphragmatic breaths, focusing on the sensation of the air moving in and out of your body.

This is a gentle yet powerful exercise that can help activate the parasympathetic nervous system and promote feelings of relaxation and calm. By shifting your attention between different sensations in your body, you're encouraging your nervous system to "pendulate" between states of activation and relaxation.

Titration on the other hand, involves gradually exposing yourself to the challenging emotions that you've tucked away in your subconscious. This, I can liken to you cooking an intricate dish on the stove. If you were to throw all the ingredients together, the overall flavor of the dish would be overwhelming. But, if you took the time to carefully add each ingredient, you'd wind up with something satiating and satisfying.

If you are in therapy, this might look like your therapist asking you to recall the event while helping you with the tools you need to gradually become more comfortable with the experience. The thing about traumatic experiences is that they require a rather delicate approach. Taking things slowly and gradually is much more helpful and productive. With time and patience, the nervous system becomes more comfortable, and you can work on healing your trauma and leading a satisfying and fulfilling life.

Here is yet another example of a titration technique that you can try:

Step 1: Settle into Your Body

Sit or lie down in a comfortable position. Take a few moments to connect with your body and notice any physical sensations that are present. Allow your breath to deepen as you bring your attention inward naturally.

Step 2: Choose a Sensation to Work With

Identify a sensation that feels present and noticeable in your body. It could be a tingling, warmth, tension, or any other sensation that you can clearly discern. Select a sensation that is not too overwhelming but still noticeable.

Step 3: Gradually Increase the Sensation

Focus your attention on the chosen sensation and imagine turning up a dial or increasing its volume. Visualize the sensation gradually increasing in intensity, but stay within a comfortable range. Notice how the sensation changes as you turn up the dial.

Step 4: Observe and Connect

As the sensation intensifies, observe how your body responds. Pay attention to any thoughts, emotions, or memories that arise. Take a moment to connect with these experiences without judgment, simply allowing them to be present.

Step 5: Gradually Decrease the Sensation

When you feel ready, imagine turning down the dial or decreasing the intensity of the sensation. Visualize the sensation gradually returning to its original level or becoming more subtle.

Step 6: Observe and Reflect

As the sensation decreases, observe any shifts or changes that occur within your body and mind. Reflect on the experience and notice how your relationship with the sensation may have transformed through the process of titration.

Step 7: Repeat and Explore Further

If you feel comfortable, you can repeat the titration process with the same or different sensations. Explore different variations and notice how your body responds. Over time, you can develop a greater sense of mastery and regulation over your bodily experiences.

Recognizing How Trauma Leaves The Body Using Sequencing Tools

When we experience trauma, our bodies tend to carry the physical and emotional memory of the event long after it has happened. While there are various therapeutic approaches to addressing trauma, sequencing tools have been found to be particularly helpful in recognizing how trauma leaves our bodies. Sequencing tools typically involve a series of physical movements that help us tune into our bodies by becoming more aware of our sensations and emotions in learning to identify the patterns of tension and release that are connected to past trauma.

Yoga is one of the most popular sequencing tools, and the best part about it is that there are so many platforms like YouTube and Pocket Yoga that give you the freedom to practice anytime, anywhere! It has numerous benefits for our mental health, including the ability to alleviate some of our anxiety symptoms. And perhaps more importantly, it has the ability to help us reconnect with and become more aware of our bodies and the discomfort that sometimes lives within us.

Another sequencing tool is TRE, also known as tension and trauma-releasing exercises, which is a body-based approach to releasing tension and trauma. It involves a series of simple exercises that help activate the body's natural tremoring mechanism. You might be wondering, what's trembling? Well, it's actually a natural reflex that animals use to discharge stress and tension from their bodies. Think of a dog shaking itself vigorously after a scary encounter—that's tremoring in action!

So, when we experience stress or trauma, our bodies often hold onto that energy, causing tension and discomfort. TRE aims to help us release this stored energy by inducing tremors in a controlled and safe way. By engaging in specific exercises and positions, we can activate these tremors and allow the body to release the built-up tension.

Tremors may sound a bit intimidating, but they're actually quite gentle and can feel quite pleasant. It's like a gentle vibration or shaking that starts from within and gradually spreads throughout your body. During this process, you are invited to pay attention to your body's sensations, allowing the tremors to flow and release any tension or trauma that might be stored. It's really a self-empowering practice that encourages us to listen to your body's wisdom and release what no longer serves us.

Let's have a look at a practical TRE exercise that you can try:

- Stand up or sit in a chair with your feet flat on the ground, hip-width apart.
- Take a couple of deep breaths and feel your feet connected to the ground.
- Slowly begin to shake your right leg, allowing the shaking to spread up through your thigh and into your hip.
- As the shaking intensifies, allow your right arm/hand to join the shaking.
- Pay attention to any sensations or emotions that arise, but try to avoid analyzing them or getting caught up in any stories they may trigger.
- Allow the shaking to continue for at least a minute or until it naturally subsides.
- Rest for a few moments before repeating the exercise with your left leg/arm.

Trauma can be complex and nuanced, so we should always remember that it's important to address it with care and compassion. Addressing it with the appropriate resources and help can help us heal and move forward. An approach that works or works for someone else may not necessarily be the same thing that works for you. Ask for help along the way, and it's certainly something that you don't have to navigate all on your own. In the next chapter, we explore the different approaches that we can take when navigating trauma from anxiety, PTSD, addiction, and coping mechanisms. So, take a breath, and when you're ready, dive right in.

4

Somatic Therapy for Specific Challenges

"Trauma creates changes you don't choose. Healing is about creating change that you do choose."

— UNKNOWN

Trauma is like a tangled web of emotions, memories, and reactions that requires careful consideration and tailored approaches for healing and recovery.

Think of it as a puzzle with various pieces scattered all around. Each piece represents a specific challenge or aspect of the traumatic experience. Just as no two puzzles are exactly the same, no two individuals' traumas are identical either. That's why a one-size-fits-all approach simply doesn't cut it when it comes to addressing trauma.

Imagine two people who have experienced similar traumatic events— let's say a car accident. While the event itself may be similar, the emotional reactions, coping mechanisms, and support systems can vary significantly between the two. One person may develop anxiety and struggle with driving again, while the other might experience flashbacks and nightmares. It's crucial to acknowledge and understand these differences.

To effectively navigate and find support throughout trauma recovery, we need to consider our unique challenges and preferences. Some people benefit from talking therapies like counseling or psychotherapy, where they can explore their feelings and work through emotional turmoil. Others might find solace in creative outlets such as art therapy or music therapy, which allow them to express themselves non-verbally.

It's about finding the thing that makes us feel most empowered individuals to take an active role in our healing journey. It's about Flexibility and adaptability as we learn to find our way through this complex maze of emotions and challenges. It's not easy finding the right approach, but together we'll navigate the options, and there are for us. We are, after all, in this together.

Improving Body Image and Self-Esteem

I know that I am not the only one who struggles with this question: how do I accept my body? Especially when so many messages are floating around about how we should or shouldn't look—so many messages about what is and isn't acceptable. But I have found a way of working on this issue. I have discovered that I can do this by realizing that anytime a thought or belief about my body pops out that tries to hurt me, it simply isn't true. And that when I allow myself to feel these emotions that these thoughts release from me, they leave a whole lot of room open for acceptance. And joy. And love. And peace as well.

I want you to think of a beautiful and vibrant space filled with flowers, plants, and trees. Each element represents a different aspect of our self-image and self-esteem. Now, envision that this garden has been neglected and experienced a harsh storm in the past, leaving it damaged and struggling to flourish.

In this metaphor, our body image is like a delicate flower. It represents how we perceive and feel about our physical appearance. When we have a poor body image, it's as if the flower's petals are wilted and drooping. We may feel dissatisfied, critical, or even disgusted with how our bodies look. Negative thoughts and comparisons can cloud our perception, preventing us from appreciating our unique beauty.

Next, let's consider our self-esteem as a towering tree within the garden. This tree symbolizes our overall sense of self-worth, confidence, and the belief we have in our abilities. With low self-esteem, the branches of the tree become weak and fragile. We doubt ourselves, constantly seek validation from others, and struggle to assert our needs and boundaries. Our self-esteem becomes vulnerable to external influences, leaving us feeling small and insignificant.

Trauma can be likened to the storm that ravaged the garden in the past. Just as a storm damages plants and disrupts their growth, traumatic experiences can deeply impact our body image and self-esteem. Trauma can shatter our sense of safety, trust, and control. It leaves emotional scars that distort the way we view ourselves.

For example, if body shaming or physical abuse were things that you were subjected to, it can lead to distorted body image and self-esteem issues. The negative messages or actions from the past become internalized, creating a toxic narrative that echoes in our minds. We may carry shame, guilt, or a deep-rooted sense of unworthiness as a result. Trauma can impair our ability to form healthy connections with others. It can make us feel isolated, detached, or unworthy of love and acceptance. These feelings further contribute to low self-esteem, reinforcing the negative cycle.

Let's take a look at some of the exercises that you can try to help you improve your self-esteem and self-image through somatic exercises.

Authentic Movement: Authentic movement involves allowing your body to move spontaneously without judgment or conscious control. By tuning into your body's impulses and sensations, you can explore your relationship with movement and better understand your body's capabilities and needs. This technique promotes self-acceptance and fosters a positive body image. A typical example would look like this:

- You sit with your eyes closed and bring your attention to your breath and bodily sensations.
- I sit quietly nearby, holding a safe and attentive space for you.
- You allow your body to move spontaneously, without conscious direction or influence.
- The movement takes any form or quality, such as shaking, twisting, reaching, or stillness.
- You stay present with your experience, noticing any emotions, thoughts, or physical sensations that arise as you move.
- I observe the movement with curiosity and compassion without offering feedback, interpretation, or influence.
- When the movement feels complete, you gradually slow down and come to a stillness.
- We may share any insights or reflections that emerged during the process, but this is not necessary.

Body Mapping: Body mapping involves using art materials to visually represent your body. It offers a pathway to reconnecting with our physical selves. By engaging in a creative and introspective process, we can unlock a deeper understanding of our bodies, emotions, and experiences. Here's how you can do that:

Gathering Supplies: Gather various art supplies such as paper, markers, colored pencils, or paints. Choose materials that resonate with you and inspire your creativity. Find a quiet and comfortable space where you can freely express yourself without distractions.

The Journey: Sit or lie down in a relaxed position, taking a few deep breaths to center yourself. Close your eyes and bring your attention to your body. Notice any sensations, tensions, or emotions that arise. Allow yourself to fully immerse in the present moment. When you feel ready, gently open your eyes and let your artistic intuition guide you as you begin the process of body mapping.

Exploring Your Body's Landscape: Take a moment to observe your body. Start by tracing the outline of your body on the paper, creating a basic silhouette. Then, begin to add details and symbols that represent different aspects of your physical and emotional experiences. Notice any areas that draw your attention, such as scars, birthmarks, or areas of tension. Use colors, shapes, and textures to express the sensations and emotions associated with each part of your body.

Reflecting and Unveiling: Once you have completed your body map, take a step back and observe the artwork as a whole. Reflect on the symbols, colors, and shapes you have incorporated. What messages are your body and emotions conveying through this expressive creation? Allow yourself to connect with the deeper meanings that emerge, embracing any insights or revelations that arise from this exploration.

Embracing Self-Compassion: As you engage with your body map, practice self-compassion and non-judgment. Embrace the uniqueness of your body and honor its journey. Notice any areas of tension or discomfort, and send love and acceptance to those parts. Offer gratitude for the strength and resilience your body carries. This practice fosters self-acceptance, appreciation, and a sense of harmony between body, mind, and spirit.

A few final words from me to you: Embrace this powerful tool, and may it guide you toward a more embodied and authentic existence.

Somatic Dialogue: Somatic dialogue involves having a conversation with your body. When we enter a somatic inquiry, we want to cultivate a sensory language with our own bodies to discover what guidance and truths exist deeply within them. Learning how to deepen that dialogue with the body can take practice and a lot of time, but it is possible to rewrite your inner dialogue with yourself.

You can consciously create a friendlier and more explorative relationship with your internal dialogue and emotions.

Catch the thought and say the exact opposite to yourself. Essentially instead of saying something like *I am so unattractive. I could be smaller around the hips or waist.* You can shift the script to something more like *I am beautiful. I know that it's hard to see or even believe that right now, but I have this body that holds dear life. I get to and will appreciate all its remarkable contours.*

Practice saying loving and kind, and encouraging things to yourself regularly. I am a remarkable person. *I love myself for who I am. I appreciate this body for all that it does for me. Instead of spending time trying to hate it, I will work on building a loving and kind relationship with it.*

Replace any judgment that you have of yourself with more compassion and care. Example: *I hate that I did,* can be reframed to: *I don't like how I responded to this particular situation. I'm still learning how to respond differently, so I will give myself a lot of grace along the way.*

Courageously continue ahead on the road to emotional recovery and self-love with a whole lot of self-love. Do the work. Choose love. Choose to learn; choose to heal. Choose to say things differently to yourself. Every time and every day. Of finding a spot. Sit quietly, close your eyes, and ask your body questions like, "What do you need from me?" or "How can I nurture and support you?" Listen for any sensations, emotions, or images that arise in response.

You're not going to love your body every day; you're not always going to love how your tummy folds when you sit or how you sometimes get a double chin when you laugh., but you can choose acceptance and appreciation over self-criticism. We recognize that our bodies are unique and undergo various changes as we age. Instead of constantly striving for a flawless appearance, we can focus on embracing our imperfections and nurturing a healthy relationship with our bodies.

Societal standards of beauty are often unrealistic and unattainable. The media bombards us with images of airbrushed and photoshopped models, creating an unattainable ideal that only perpetuates self-doubt and insecurity. By choosing acceptance and seeing ourselves in a more positive light, we allow ourselves to let go of the constant need for perfection and comparison. We can shift our perspective toward gratitude for our bodies' abilities and the experiences they have carried us through. Our bodies are not merely objects to be judged; they are vessels that allow us to explore the world, connect with others, and experience life's joys.

Choosing acceptance also extends beyond our physical appearance. It involves embracing our unique personalities, quirks, and talents. By valuing our inner qualities and focusing on personal growth, we can cultivate a sense of confidence and self-assurance that radiates from within. The journey toward body acceptance is ongoing and requires patience and self-compassion. It's normal to have days where we struggle with negative thoughts. Still, by actively challenging those thoughts and replacing them with positive affirmations, we can gradually shift our mindset toward self-acceptance.

You are more than the sum of your physical attributes. You are a complex and beautiful individual deserving of love and acceptance.

Working With Anxiety and Panic Attacks

Living with anxiety and panic attacks can be a challenging and overwhelming experience, but through somatic therapy, there is hope.

Think of your mind as a bustling city, with thoughts and emotions buzzing through its streets. Anxiety is like a persistent traffic jam that disrupts the flow of your mental landscape. It's a state of heightened worry and unease, often accompanied by physical sensations like a racing heart or tense muscles. It's like having a constant, nagging passenger in your car, questioning every decision you make and amplifying your concerns. The traffic of anxiety can make it difficult to focus, relax, or enjoy life's journey.

Panic attacks on the other hand, are like intense storms that strike without warning. Imagine being on a serene beach, basking in the sun, and suddenly dark clouds gather and unleash a torrential downpour. Panic attacks are similar—they bring a surge of overwhelming fear and discomfort that can be paralyzing. It's as if a lightning bolt of anxiety strikes, triggering a cascade of alarming thoughts and physical symptoms. Your heart races like thunder, your breath becomes shallow and rapid as if caught in a gusty wind, and you may even experience chest pain or dizziness. Panic attacks are like being caught in a turbulent storm that engulfs your entire being, leaving you feeling out of control and desperate for shelter.

It's easy to confuse anxiety and panic attacks with one another, but they're actually quite different. Anxiety is a general state of worry and apprehension that can persist over time. Panic attacks, on the other hand, are sudden and intense bursts of fear that come and go relatively quickly.

Another difference lies in their triggers. Anxiety can arise from various sources like work, relationships, or future uncertainties, while panic attacks often seem to emerge out of nowhere without any apparent trigger. Panic attacks can even occur without an immediate threat, making them feel even more disorienting.

When it comes to tackling anxiety and panic attacks, it's essential to have a toolbox filled with helpful techniques. Think of it like having a utility belt with gadgets to combat a variety of issues. Here are a few techniques you can try:

Deep Breathing

Take a moment to focus on your breath. Imagine you're inflating a balloon in your belly as you inhale slowly through your nose. Then exhale through your mouth, letting go of tension and stress. Deep breathing helps activate the body's relaxation response, calming both the body and mind.

Cognitive Restructuring

I want you to think of cognitive restructuring as a skilled forest guide accompanying you on a journey through a dense forest. The guide helps you navigate the tangled paths of your mind, challenging and reshaping your thoughts about the forest. Instead of seeing every rustle as a sign of impending doom, they encourage us to consider alternative explanations, like perhaps it's just a harmless squirrel or a gentle breeze stirring the leaves.

In panic attacks and anxiety, cognitive restructuring involves identifying and challenging negative, distorted, or catastrophic thoughts that contribute to heightened anxiety. It helps us develop a more balanced and realistic perspective on our fears and triggers. By examining the evidence and evaluating the accuracy of your thoughts, we can reframe them in a way that reduces anxiety and promotes a sense of control.

For example, during a panic attack, a thought like, *"I'm going to die!"* might pop up. Cognitive restructuring would involve questioning the validity of this thought and exploring alternative explanations. You might ask yourself, *"What evidence do I have to support this belief? Have I experienced a similar situation before without any harm?"* By examining the evidence and challenging irrational thoughts, you gradually replace them with more rational and calming ones, such as *"I've gotten through panic attacks before, and I know they won't last forever."*

Cognitive restructuring is particularly helpful because it addresses the root cause: thoughts and interpretations. It empowers us to take an active role in managing our anxiety by recognizing and modifying unhelpful patterns of thinking. By reshaping the cognitive landscape, we create a more resilient mindset that allows us to navigate life's challenges with greater confidence and calmness.

Self-Care

Self-care is a lot of things. Some days it looks like reading a book. On other days it's meditation or eating a balanced meal. It's taking time to go to therapy, looking after your body, mind, and spirit. It's using your voice and empowering yourself to heal. It's beautiful and messy but so, so necessary. And when it comes to managing anxiety and panic attacks, self-care becomes an essential lifeline, a gentle anchor in the stormy sea of our emotions. It acts as our sturdy anchor in these moments, keeping us grounded and steady amidst the chaos. It provides a sense of stability and security, allowing us to weather the storm and find our way back to calmer waters.

Self-care is empowering because it reminds us that we deserve care, compassion, and gentleness, especially during times of heightened anxiety. Just as a weary traveler seeks refuge in a cozy inn after a long and challenging journey, self-care offers a haven to rest, rejuvenate, and recharge.

Engaging in self-care activities tailored to your needs can help you regain a sense of control over your anxiety. It's like building a personalized toolkit with strategies and practices supporting your well-being. Maybe your toolkit includes deep breathing exercises that help calm your racing heart during a panic attack. Or perhaps it includes journaling, where you pour your thoughts and worries onto paper, freeing your mind from their weight.

It also isn't a one-size-fits-all solution. It's a unique and personal journey that requires exploration and experimentation. It's about discovering what brings you comfort, joy, and tranquility. It's about permitting yourself to prioritize your needs and carve out time for activities that nourish your soul.

It isn't selfish; it will never be. Taking care of yourself allows you to show up fully in your life—as it should be. So, embrace it because you're building the foundation for a healthier, happier, and more balanced life.

Here's a list of self-care suggestions

- deep breathing exercises
- meditation
- taking a warm bath or shower
- practicing yoga or gentle stretching
- going for a walk in nature
- listening to calming music or nature sounds
- writing in a journal or practicing gratitude
- engaging in a creative hobby, such as painting or knitting
- reading a book or listening to an audiobook
- trying aromatherapy with essential oils like lavender or chamomile
- having a cup of herbal tea or warm milk before bed
- spending quality time with a beloved pet

- watching a funny or uplifting movie or TV show
- trying progressive muscle relaxation techniques
- engaging in mindful eating by savoring each bite of a favorite meal
- pampering yourself with a face mask or a DIY spa day
- practicing positive affirmations or self-affirming statements
- disconnecting from technology and spending time in solitude
- engaging in a hobby that brings you joy, such as gardening or playing a musical instrument
- seeking support from a therapist, counselor, or support group

Managing anxiety and panic attacks is a journey; what works for one person may not work for another. It's all about finding the techniques that resonate with you and building your superhero toolkit. Be patient with yourself, celebrate small victories, and know that you can gain control over anxiety and panic attacks with time and practice.

Healing From Trauma and PTSD

Healed people aren't just the ones with smiles constantly pasted on their faces; they are the ones who, despite all they've been through, still possess the strength and the willingness to sit through all their difficult emotions. It's a lot of things too. Sometimes it looks like teardrops on a page. A playlist on an empty road during a road trip. Other times it's a painful goodbye or a new hello. It looks different from all of us, but the one thing that it isn't is the glamorous portrayal often seen in popular culture. This is especially true when healing involves emotional or psychological wounds.

Healing is deeply personal. Something that requires taking the time to look inward and acknowledge the pain that we've experienced. It's about sitting with that pain, understanding its root cause, and then working through it bit by bit. This process is often slow and painstaking, and there's no shortcut or quick fix. There's often a misconception that it is a linear process. Once you start, you're on a steady path toward wholeness. But this couldn't be further from the truth. Healing is messy. It's a rollercoaster ride of highs and lows, of forward progress and setbacks. Some days you feel like you've made leaps and bounds, and other days, it feels like you've regressed.

We live in a culture of instant gratification, where we're used to getting what we want instantly. But healing doesn't work that way. You can't rush it. You have to give your body and mind the time they need to recover, and that takes patience. On top of that, it involves confronting uncomfortable truths about ourselves and our experiences. It can mean facing our fears, our insecurities, and our self-doubt. It can mean accepting responsibility for our actions and learning to forgive ourselves for our mistakes. This is hard, painful work, and it cannot be glossed over or glamorized.

It's the process by which we come to terms with our past, learn from our experiences, and move forward with our lives. It's the process that allows us to grow, to change, to become better versions of ourselves. And in that sense, it's one of the most important journeys we can embark on.

Trauma is not just a mental experience but also impacts our physical bodies. So, let's explore some specific types of somatic therapy that can be helpful in this context.

Somatic Experiencing (SE): Picture this—you're watching a suspenseful movie, and your heart starts pounding, your palms get all sweaty, and your muscles tense up. These bodily sensations exemplify our natural "fight or flight" response. Somatic Experiencing helps us release that stored trauma energy by gently guiding us to notice and regulate these physical sensations. It's like giving the body permission to complete the response that got stuck during the traumatic event.

One thing about the body is that it will always choose what's familiar over a peace that feels unfamiliar. We know that our earliest experiences shape and affect the wiring of our brains. Still, a bit too often, we rarely realize that these experiences are altogether unhealthy, harmful, and neglectful to our own well-being. Our system becomes so conditioned to it and even chooses a dynamic that replicates that same feeling matter how healthy or supportive a new relationship might be. We'll be logically telling ourselves that we want that while the system does its own thing and says: *"I have no idea what to do with that". I don't know how to trust that. That's a feeling I have never known."*

As a result, our systems send us alarm signals through anxiety, self-doubt, anxiety, and intrusive thoughts. For example, we may go into this state when we enter a new relationship and retrieve information about the mother figure that was emotionally abusive or overly critical or the unavailable father and unconsciously be reminded that it's normal. Or perhaps, We'll be reminded of the high stress and intensity that we experienced in our households while growing up—the things that make us find partners who are safe and secure, "boring."

EMDR: Picture yourself as a librarian for a moment; you're organizing a library filled with all of the memories of your life. Each memory is stored on a bookshelf, tucked away in the pages of one of those books, but some of these memories carry heavy emotional weight due to traumatic experiences. Now, EMDR is like having a badass assistant who helps you reorganize and process those heavy books in a way that reduces their emotional intensity. This assistant is what we call Bilateral Stimulation (BS).

BS can take various forms, but let us imagine it as a pair of gentle hands that flip through the pages of the memory books, one page at a time. As these hands move back and forth, it's as if they are gently tapping into your brain's natural healing powers. During an EMDR session, you choose a specific traumatic memory to work on. You take that memory book off the shelf and hold it in your hands, allowing the vivid details and emotions to surface.

Now, here comes the magic. You begin to create bilateral stimulation, such as moving your fingers from side to side, using light and sound. As your eyes move back and forth, your brain enters a unique state of focused attention. This bilateral stimulation activates both hemispheres of the brain, facilitating the processing of the traumatic memory in a controlled and safe environment.

As the pages turn, you may start to notice something remarkable happening. The emotional intensity of the memory gradually diminishes. The vivid colors and vivid emotions that once overwhelmed you begin to fade, like ink slowly fading on a page.

The bilateral stimulation helps your brain make new connections and associations with the traumatic memory. It's as if the librarian assistant is reorganizing the shelves, placing the memory book in a different section of the library alongside other books that evoke more positive emotions and resilience. Over time, with repeated EMDR sessions, the memory book becomes less distressing and more manageable. The emotional weight it once carried is significantly reduced, allowing you to view the memory from a new perspective. It's like transforming a heavy, burdensome book into a lighter paperback edition. In this way, EMDR and bilateral stimulation assist in processing traumatic memories by stimulating your brain's natural ability to heal. By reorganizing and reducing the emotional intensity of these memories, EMDR helps you integrate the traumatic experiences into your life to promote healing, resilience, and a renewed sense of empowerment.

It makes your memory a place where you can navigate and explore your life's story with greater ease and emotional well-being.

Dance/Movement Therapy: Movement, any kind of movement, is liberating and healing, and who says therapy can't be fun? Dance/-Movement Therapy is all about telling your story through the language of dance. It is a language that transcends words, allowing you to express emotions that are otherwise difficult to express. It's a sanctuary that allows you to channel your emotions, energy, and creativity into movements that share something meaningful. When it comes to trauma and PTSD, dance and movement provide a safe and expressive outlet for us to explore and release emotions, sensations, and memories. Let's have a look at an example of how it would work

We have Jane in this scenario, who was in a car accident that has left her with deep emotional and physical scars. Now she feels anxious and disconnected from her body, and memories of the accident often trigger panic attacks. Jane decided to explore somatic therapy as a part of her healing process. As a part of her practice, she decided to engage in gentle movement exercises. It was simple movements like deep breathing, stretching, or grounding exercises to help her establish a sense of safety and connection with her body. As she grew more comfortable, she started to introduce more expressive movements like allowing her body to move freely, without judgment, shame, or a specific technique—giving herself permission to explore her emotions through the movement. This involved swaying, shaking, and dancing to release tension and energy stored in her body.

Throughout her practice, Jane learned to notice those sensations, emotions, and memories that arose. She guided herself to pay attention to the physical sensations in her body, such as tightness in her chest or a knot in her stomach, and to express those sensations through her movements. Dance and movement is what gradually allowed her to reconnect with her body and access her inner resources for healing. Over time, she might notice reduced anxiety and an increased sense of empowerment. She could release the traumatic energy trapped in her body through movement and replace it with a newfound sense of strength and resilience.

In this way, dance and movement provide a non-verbal pathway for us to process and integrate our traumatic experiences.

Trauma Release Exercises (TRE): Remember that "fight-or-flight" response we mentioned earlier? Well, TRE taps into our body's innate ability to shake off stress and tension. Performing a series of simple exercises, such as gentle tremors and stretches, allows the body to release stored trauma energy. It's like giving your body a good shake to let go of the past.

Unleash and Release: A Short Tension and Trauma Releasing Exercise (TRE)

This exercise aims to help you tap into your body's innate ability to release stress and tension. These simple and gentle movements will encourage the natural tremoring response that facilitates the release of stored tension.

Step 1: Grounding

Start by finding a quiet and secure space where you can fully engage in this practice without any interruptions. Stand with your feet shoulder-width apart, feeling the connection between your feet and the ground beneath you. Take a moment to center yourself, bringing your attention to the present moment and the intention of releasing any stored tension.

Step 2: Gentle Shaking

Begin by gently shaking your body from the feet up through the legs, hips, torso, arms, and hands. Allow the shaking to start softly and gradually increase in intensity. Feel the vibrations moving through your body, loosening and releasing any held tension. Trust the natural wisdom of your body as it begins to unwind and let go. Embrace the freedom of movement and surrender to the process.

Step 3: Grounding Pause

After a few minutes of shaking, come to a still-standing position and pause. Feel the sensations in your body and notice any shifts or changes. Take a few deep breaths, allowing yourself to fully integrate the experience. This pause is essential for grounding and reconnecting with your body. Observe any emotions or sensations that may arise without judgment, simply acknowledging them.

Step 4: Self-Care

Now, take a moment for self-care. Place your hands on your heart or any areas of your body that may require attention or support. Offer yourself compassion and gratitude for engaging in this practice. Take deep breaths, allowing the breath to nourish and heal your body. Recognize that you have taken an important step toward releasing and healing stored tension.

These are just a few examples of the diverse range of somatic therapy types available for trauma and PTSD that we have mentioned. Each approach offers a unique pathway to healing tailored to the individual's needs. Incorporating somatic therapy into your trauma recovery can be an empowering and transformative experience. So, take a deep breath, trust in your body's wisdom, and embark on healing!

Addiction and Compulsive Behaviors

Addiction is like wallpaper covering up our brokenness, fears, and dissociations. It makes it so, so much harder to do what we need to do, which is: to connect. It's a barrier that disconnects us from the world, from our loved ones, and, most critically, from ourselves.

The crux of the matter is that addiction creates a false sense of security. During our pain and our struggles, it offers an illusion of comfort, a refuge from an often harsh reality. It's a siren song that lures us away from the path of self-discovery and healing.

But the reality is that this refuge is a mirage. In the long run, it does more harm than good. It isolates us and creates a chasm between who we truly are and who we present to the world. It's like a mask that hides our true selves, not only from the world but from ourselves as well, making self-acceptance and self-love seemingly impossible feats.

It's important to remember that while addiction may be a formidable opponent, it is not invincible. Breaking free from its grip requires us to confront our demons, to rip off that wallpaper and stare at the brokenness beneath. It's a difficult journey, no doubt, but it's also a journey worth undertaking. Because to connect—to truly connect with ourselves and others—we must first be willing to face our fears, our pain, and our dissociations. We must be willing to stand in the face of our vulnerability and say: "I am not perfect, and that's okay."

Addition and compulsive behaviors are rooted in unresolved trauma. Be that emotional or physical Somatic therapy helps to address these underlying issues by helping us identify and release the patterns of tension and movement that are holding us back from healing from the trauma.

One of how bodily therapy is used in addiction treatment is by helping identify and manage the cravings. Cravings are undeniably one of the most challenging aspects of addiction and something that most people find to be so overwhelming. Somatic therapy helps you identify the physical sensations accompanying the cravings and teaches you to tolerate and manage them healthier. This is incredibly empowering because it helps you to feel less controlled by the cravings and more in control of your body.

Also, it helps you release the emotions that are stored in these emotions. The techniques used are incredibly transformative because they help you connect on the deepest level possible with the root causes of the compulsive behaviors.

Earlier on, we established that somatic experiencing is a technique that recognizes our minds and bodies' interconnectedness. By gently exploring bodily sensations and allowing the body's natural healing process to unfold, you allow yourself to find relief from the grip of addiction and compulsive disorder. Let's look at a practical example

Meet Amaraah. She has been struggling with alcohol addiction for years. Whenever she feels stressed or overwhelmed, she immediately reaches for a drink, using alcohol as a coping mechanism. Amaraah wants to break free from this destructive cycle and regain control of her life, so she decides to look into somatic experiences as a way to help her heal.

The starting point for her is to focus on her breath. This is where she learns to tune into her body and notice any physical sensations that arise. What she then starts to feel is a tightness in her chest and a heaviness in her gut. These sensations have always been triggers for her alcohol cravings. Slowly and patiently, she learns to explore these sensations without judgment, allowing herself to be present with her body's responses.

As she continues to focus on her physical sensations, memories from her past surface. She recalls a childhood incident where she felt neglected and unseen by her parents. The memory is what triggers that surge of emotions and a desire to escape reality through the bottle. She learns to acknowledge her emotions with grace and observes how her body responds to this memory. This is also where she learns that these sensations are not something to be feared but rather an opportunity for healing.

As she progresses throughout her practice, she dives deeper into the emotions and physical manifestations. She notices her shoulders tensing up and her breath becoming shallow. Gradually, she learns to release the tension in her shoulders and take deep, grounding breaths.

Through this process, Amarrah begins to notice a shift within herself. Her intense craving starts to subside, and she experiences a newfound sense of calm and empowerment. She realizes that she doesn't need to rely on alcohol to escape her emotions; she can acknowledge and process them healthily.

Over subsequent somatic experiencing sessions, Amaraah dives deeper into her past traumas and explores the sensations associated with her addiction triggers. Each time, she gains more insight into the underlying causes of her addiction and develops healthier coping mechanisms. She gradually learns to regulate her nervous system and reconnect with her body's innate healing ability. She becomes more resilient in the face of stress, and her cravings for alcohol diminish significantly.

By addressing the root causes of her addiction on a bodily level, she no longer feels controlled by her cravings. She now has the tools to navigate life's challenges without relying on substances. It offered a path to healing that went beyond traditional talk therapy, providing a holistic approach to recovery.

Managing Depression and Low Mood

Trauma can leave a lasting impact on our mental well-being, sometimes leading to depression and low mood. It's like a dark cloud that hangs over our minds, making it difficult to see the sunshine. But how does trauma connect to the state of our moods?

You see when a traumatic event occurs, it can shake us to our core. It may make us feel scared, helpless, or overwhelmed. These intense emotions can disrupt the delicate balance of chemicals in our brains, affecting our mood. It's like throwing a wrench into the gears of a well-oiled machine. Trauma often alters our perception of the world. It can make us lose trust in others or constantly feel on edge as if danger is lurking around every corner. This hypervigilance and negative outlook can drain our energy and contribute to feelings of sadness and hopelessness.

It's like a heavy backpack we carry around. It weighs us down, making every step harder. We might isolate ourselves from loved ones, lose interest in activities we once enjoyed, or struggle to find motivation in daily life. All these are factors that can gradually lead to depression and a persistent low mood.

While depression and low mood may seem similar, there are some key differences between the two. Let's say you wake up feeling a bit down, maybe your favorite cereal is out of stock, or you had a rough night's sleep. It's normal to experience a low mood occasionally, and it's usually triggered by specific events or circumstances. A low mood is like a passing cloud that can come and go, affecting your emotions for a short period of time. It's similar to feeling a little blue or having a temporary dip in your spirits.

Depression is a more persistent and prolonged state of feeling low. It's like a dark cloud that lingers over you for an extended period, often lasting weeks, months, or even longer. Unlike low mood, depression doesn't necessarily have an obvious cause or trigger. It can seep into various aspects of your life, affecting your thoughts, emotions, and daily functioning.

Another distinction that we should look at is how each one affects our daily lives. Low mood might bring about temporary disruptions in your routine or productivity, but it doesn't typically interfere with your ability to carry out daily tasks. Depression, on the other hand, often leads to significant impairment in various areas of life, such as work, relationships, and self-care. It can make even the simplest tasks feel overwhelming and exhausting.

Breathwork, meditation, and body scanning are all somatic therapy techniques that can be used to manage these states. I've provided examples of these exercises in Chapter 2, so you can refer back to it if you want to regroup and recenter yourself. But here is also an example of another breathwork exercise that you can use to regroup and regather the pieces of yourself:

Tranquil Breath: A Step-by-Step Somatic Therapy Exercise

This is an exercise designed to bring deep relaxation and inner harmony.

Step 1: Settling In

Begin by finding a quiet space where you can fully immerse yourself in this practice. Sit or lie down in a comfortable position, ensuring your body is relaxed and supported. Take a moment to let go of any external distractions and focus solely on your breath.

Step 2: Awareness of Breath

Bring your attention to your breath without attempting to change it. Notice the gentle rise and fall of your abdomen or the sensation of air flowing in and out of your nostrils. Observe the quality and rhythm of your breath, anchoring your awareness in the present moment. Allow any thoughts or worries to gently drift away as you fully embrace this present experience.

Step 3: Deepening the Breath

Now, take a slow, deep breath in through your nose, allowing your abdomen to expand with each inhale. Feel the air filling your lungs, bringing vitality and energy. Exhale slowly through your mouth, releasing any tension or stress. Each breath deepens your relaxation, nurturing a sense of calm within. Continue this pattern, focusing on the soothing rhythm of your breath.

Step 4: Counting the Breath

To further enhance your breath awareness, begin counting your breath cycles. Inhale deeply, counting silently to yourself. Then, exhale for the same count. For example, inhale to the count of four, and exhale to the count of four. This simple technique cultivates focus and steadies the mind. If your attention wanders, gently bring it back to the count, allowing yourself to sink deeper into relaxation.

Step 5: Breath Expansion

Now, let's explore breath expansion. Inhale deeply, feeling your breath expand from your abdomen to your chest, allowing your ribcage to gently widen. As you exhale, visualize releasing any residual tension or negativity. With each breath, imagine your body becoming lighter, freer, and more at ease. Continue this expansive breath, feeling a sense of spaciousness within your being.

The body needs time. Time to process, time to detox. The body needs time to heal from the painful things we sometimes experience. So, give it the time that it needs to recover. You are going to be okay. It might not feel like it right now, but believe me, and you really will.

5

Integrating Somatic Therapy With Other Modalities

"Healing work is supposed to stretch the nervous system, not stress it."

— CHER HAMPTON

Integrating somatic therapy with other types of therapy is like weaving together a tapestry of healing modalities, with each thread contributing to its unique texture and hue to the finished piece. Just imagine yourself standing in front of a loom, selecting a thread that reflects the diversity of people—each one a reflection of an aspect of their journey toward wholeness.

Somatic therapy is powerful because of the emphasis that it places on the mind-body connection. Our bodies are more than vessels meant to carry us from day to day. The profound understanding that our physical sensations, movements, and postures are closely intertwined with our emotions, thoughts, and overall well-being has captivated me.

It is also rooted in the principles of embodiment, recognizes that our bodies possess a wisdom of their own, and that it acknowledges that traumas, stressors, and life experiences can become imprinted in our physical form, leading to a variety of psychological and emotional challenges. No single approach can fully encompass the complexity of the human experience. While Somatic Therapy provides a valuable framework, it is important to acknowledge that humans are multi-faceted beings with unique histories, cultures, and perspectives. Our experiences are diverse, and what works for one person may not necessarily work for another.

The field of therapy is rich with various modalities, each offering its own unique lens through which to understand and address human suffering. From cognitive-behavioral therapies that focus on thoughts and beliefs to psychodynamic approaches that explore the unconscious mind, each modality contributes to the vast tapestry of therapeutic practices.

Rather than adopting a one-size-fits-all approach, therapists often integrate multiple modalities and tailor their interventions to meet the specific needs of their clients. This eclectic approach allows for a flexible and dynamic therapeutic process that recognizes the intricate interplay between the mind, body, and spirit.

The field of Somatic Therapy itself also encompasses various techniques and methodologies. From traditional body-centered psychotherapy to more innovative approaches like dance therapy, yoga therapy, and sensorimotor psychotherapy, a rich tapestry of somatic modalities can be explored.

While it resonates deeply with me, I have certainly come to appreciate that it is just one thread in the vast fabric of therapeutic interventions available. The human experience is multifaceted, and our healing journeys require a nuanced and individualized approach. By embracing the diversity of therapeutic modalities, we can honor the complexity of the human experience and pave the way for transformative healing and growth.

Combining Somatic Therapy With Talk Therapy

I love that expression that says: *"We don't just think our way out of pain, we talk our way through it; we allow ourselves to feel our way through it."*

See, the natural thing to want to do when we encounter pain of any kind is to avoid it completely or to get rid of it as quickly as we can. This approach, however, rarely works; in fact, it can often make the pain worse. What is helpful, however, is to allow ourselves to feel it without judgment. In doing so, we allow ourselves to gain a deeper understanding of what's causing us the pain so that we can address it.

When we talk about our pain, we give it a voice, an outlet. This is incredibly healing because it allows us to express our emotions and feel heard and understood. In addition to that, sharing our pain is something that has the power to make us feel less alone because it allows people who have gone through similar experiences to share their journeys and how they got through it, despite feeling otherwise.

Talk therapy, also known as psychotherapy or counseling, is a form of treatment that involves talking with a trained professional to address emotional, psychological, and behavioral challenges. It provides a safe and supportive environment for you to explore your thoughts, feelings, and experiences, with the goal of improving your overall well-being.

During talk sessions, you'll be encouraged to express your concerns, fears, and struggles openly; your therapist will actively listen to you, ask thoughtful questions, and provide guidance and support without judgment. The collaborative nature of this process has several benefits

- **Emotional Support**: Talk therapy offers a non-judgmental space where you can express yourself as freely as you can. So many people often choose to internalize their pain and face it all alone because they fear being judged or shamed for their experiences. You don't have to worry about any of that. You'll be in a safe environment that is full of empathy, understanding, and validation.
- **Self-Exploration**: It encourages self-reflection and exploration of your thoughts, emotions, and behaviors. It helps you gain insight into your patterns, beliefs, and motivations, fostering self-awareness and personal growth.
- **Behavioral Change**: Talk therapy can help you change and modify the behaviors and thoughts that are continuing to harm you.. By exploring the underlying causes of your behavioral patterns, you'll be able to make your life into something that you never want to escape from.
- **Improved Relationships**: When we heal, our relationships heal as well. When we talk about and make space for the hard things, we leave enough room for our relationships to thrive and flourish.
- **Personal Empowerment**: Ever heard of that expression (taking agency over your life?) That's essentially what talk therapy allows you to do because it encourages personal responsibility and helps you regain control over your thoughts, emotions, and actions.

Incorporating Expressive Arts and Creativity Into Somatic Work

Here's a story for you about the first art show that I attended, which was, so to say, transformative. I arrived an hour and a half earlier and waited anxiously in line, eager to immerse myself in this world of creativity and beauty. As I walked through the exhibit. I was struck by the intricate sculptures and vibrant paintings that surrounded me. Each piece seemed to have a unique story to tell, a message to impart to those who took the time to listen.

But it wasn't until a particular canvas that I truly understood art's transformative power. The painting depicted this majestic waterfall, its cascading waters frozen in time on the canvas. As I gazed upon the work, I felt a sense of peace wash over me, a feeling of calm that I had never experienced before.

At that moment, the realization hit me: art heals and soothes the soul. The artist had captured the waterfall's raw power and natural beauty, bringing it to life in a way that touched something deep within me. As I continued to explore the exhibit, I found myself drawn to other pieces that spoke to me on a deep level. Each work of art had its own unique energy, its own story to tell. It allows us to connect with our emotions on a profound level, tapping into parts of ourselves that we may or may not be aware of. Whether we are the ones creating the art or simply the ones experiencing it, it's a cathartic and transformative process.

Art therapy is a unique blend of art and psychology, where the canvas becomes a portal to the soul. It provides a safe haven for you to express your deepest thoughts, emotions, and experiences through various artistic mediums such as painting, drawing, sculpting, and collage. But it goes far beyond creating pretty pictures or mastering artistic techniques. In this captivating realm, art becomes a language of its own, capable of speaking directly to the subconscious mind. It allows you to tap into your inner world, bypassing the constraints of verbal communication. When words fail, art steps in, offering a non-threatening avenue for self-expression.

Engaging in art therapy is like embarking on an adventurous journey within yourself. It encourages exploration, self-reflection, and personal growth. Through the process of creating art, you gain insight into your emotions, uncover hidden traumas, and make sense of your life experiences. It serves as a mirror that reflects inner struggles and untapped strengths. It also fosters a sense of empowerment and control. As the artist, the brush, the pencil, or the clay are yours to hold, giving you the authority to shape the narrative. You've got the freedom to experiment, make mistakes, and find beauty in imperfection. The act of creation becomes a metaphor for life itself—a reminder that even in chaos, there is potential for beauty and growth. Art therapy is a bridge that connects the conscious and unconscious realms, facilitating emotional healing, self-discovery, and self-empowerment. It embraces the belief that creativity can be a catalyst for transformation, offering solace, insight, and a newfound sense of purpose.

Art therapy and somatic work are two dynamic approaches that can beautifully intertwine to illuminate the healing process, offering a holistic method of tackling emotional and physical distress.

When combined, these therapeutic strategies create a synergistic effect. Art therapy provides a voice to the unspoken, while somatic work helps to physically release what has been emotionally revealed. For instance, a person might paint an image that evokes feelings of anxiety and then, through guided somatic practices, they can locate where this anxiety resides in their body and work toward releasing this tension.

Combining art therapy with somatic work allows for a dual process of discovery and release, of understanding and healing. It's like a dialogue between the mind and body, each contributing to a greater understanding of the self. This unique blend of therapies provides a safe space for individuals to explore their emotions, identify physical manifestations of these emotions, and work toward resolving their underlying issues in a holistic manner.

Here's an example to illustrate how these two would work together:

Georgia is a 35-year-old woman who has been experiencing symptoms of anxiety and chronic pain due to a past traumatic experience. She often struggles to express her emotions verbally and feels disconnected from her body. To address her emotional and physical challenges, she decides to try a combination of somatic therapy and art therapy on her own.

Georgia starts with somatic therapy techniques to focus on the connection between her mind and body. She begins a series of body awareness exercises in order to recognize areas of tension and discomfort and to gain a better understanding of her body's responses. Through these exercises, she becomes more aware of her physical sensations and how they relate to her emotional state.

Next, Georgia turns to art therapy to express herself and communicate her feelings. She experiments with various art materials, such as paints, pastels, and clay, allowing her subconscious to guide the creative process. Without any expectations, she finds freedom in creating art, which helps her to express her emotions and feel liberated and relieved.

As she continues to combine somatic therapy with art therapy, Georgia explores more creative ways to connect with her body and emotions. She uses movement-based somatic techniques, such as guided dance or body-focused mindfulness exercises, to delve deeper into the relationship between her mind and body.

Over time, Georgia sees significant changes in her overall well-being. She is able to release stored trauma from her body and develop healthier coping mechanisms for her anxiety and chronic pain. She also builds a greater sense of confidence and authenticity in expressing herself.

The combination of somatic therapy and art therapy provided her with a powerful and engaging therapeutic approach. By integrating body awareness exercises, creative expression, and movement-based techniques, she is able to heal both physically and emotionally, ultimately leading to a more balanced and fulfilling life.

Combining Somatic Therapy With Mindfulness and Meditation

Mindfulness, when combined with somatic work, can be a powerful agent of healing. When combined, these two create a synergistic effect that can enhance the healing process.

We know that the mind and body are interconnected, and emotional experiences can manifest as physical sensations in our bodies. Chronic stress, trauma, and unresolved emotional issues can be stored in the body, leading to physical discomfort, pain, and even illness. Mindfulness allows us to bring non-judgmental awareness to these sensations and emotions as they arise. By cultivating present-moment awareness, we can observe bodily sensations without getting caught up in the stories or judgments associated with them.

Somatic work complements mindfulness by providing a framework for exploring and resolving these bodily sensations. This approach recognizes that the body holds valuable information and wisdom that can guide us toward healing. We can access and release stored tension, trauma, and emotional blocks through somatic practices such as body scans, movement, breathwork and body-oriented therapies like somatic experiencing or sensorimotor psychotherapy.

When mindfulness and somatic work are integrated, they create a powerful feedback loop. Mindfulness helps us become more attuned to the subtle nuances of our bodily experiences, allowing us to notice tension, discomfort, or pain areas. Through somatic practices, we can then explore these sensations further, bringing mindful awareness to them and allowing them to be fully felt and processed. This integration supports the release of emotional and physical tension, promotes self-regulation, and enhances overall well-being.

The combination of mindfulness and somatic work fosters a deeper connection between the mind and body. By developing a compassionate and non-judgmental relationship with our bodily experiences, we can cultivate a sense of safety, trust, and acceptance within ourselves. This, in turn, facilitates the healing process by creating a supportive environment for transformation and growth.

An Example:

This time, I want you to meet John—a 28-year-old who's been battling with depression and anxiety for years. In an attempt to get better and heal, he decided to try somatic therapy and see how that worked out for him. When he started out on the journey, he got introduced to various breathing techniques and used resources to guide him through a meditation exercise to help him connect with his body. He started to become more aware of a tightness in his chest and an anxious feeling that had been present with him for most of his life. As time went by, he gently nudged and encouraged himself to turn his attention toward these sensations and to explore them without any judgment, just curiosity. Over time, with that compassionate guidance, he was able to link that sensation in his chest to a traumatic event that happened when he was around 14 years old. He'd never fully processed this experience and had been carrying this weight with him in his body ever since.

Slowly, and safely he started to explore the trauma, and by using a variety of interventions, he was able to discharge the energy that had been trapped in his body for so long, and by incorporating mindful practices like meditation, he integrated his experience on a deeper level and was able to create more resilience that he could tap into in the future.

With all these resources and tools available out there for us to guide us through the healing process, it's so easy to lose ourselves in the messaging of all the things that we think we should be doing to heal. It's also quite easy for us to fall into that trap of comparing our stories to the stories of those who have claimed to have found their path toward healing and feeling like we're not doing enough. Or that our progress isn't adequate enough. The truth is the healing journey is unique; you might think that one approach will work for you but find that it's the complete opposite. What's important is to cultivate an internal dialogue where you ask yourself important questions about your needs and desires. This is something that will help you recognize your own strengths and motivations to find what works for you. Allowing yourself the grace and space to be imperfect along the way can be so liberating and help us create a more authentic sense of self.

The next chapter is one that holds quite a special place for me in my heart; it's all about self-care and cultivating a somatic self-care routine. We'll be delving into what self-care is and what it means to us, and how we can integrate it into our healing.

Breathe a while, go make yourself some tea, and when you come back, we'll learn together.

6

Building a Somatic Self-Care Practice

"Take the time today to love yourself. You deserve it"

— AVINA CELESTE

Self-care is a powerful way to express love, not only to ourselves but also to the world around us. It goes beyond mere pampering or indulgence; it is a profound act of self-love and compassion that radiates outward, positively impacting our relationships, communities, and the greater world.

When we prioritize self-care, we are essentially saying "I love you" to ourselves. We recognize our worth and acknowledge that we deserve to be nurtured and cared for by engaging in activities that bring us joy and fulfillment.

Self-care is not merely about taking care of yourself physically but mentally, emotionally, and spiritually as well. We all have less-than-good days; that's one thing for sure. But taking the time to check in with ourselves and our emotions can help us identify those areas that we need to focus on the most.

It's so easy to get caught up in the bubble of our lives, so much so that we forget to fully take care of ourselves. But when we stay present and grounded, we connect better both with ourselves and with others.

Self-care is such an important part of our healing journeys (but sometimes we so easily overlook it). No matter how busy we get, or how hard it sometimes is, we have to remember to take that time for our well-being. It's necessary for our souls that we cultivate that deep sense of love and compassion for ourselves.

Developing a Personalized Somatic Self-Care Routine

Somatic self-care is a captivating dance between your body and mind, a symphony of nurturing gestures that rejuvenate your entire being. It's like a waltz of self-love, where you embrace the beauty of your physical vessel and honor its needs with tender devotion. In this enchanting journey, you become the choreographer of your own well-being. It's the art of tending to this exquisite garden, watering each blossom with intention and care. It's about listening closely to the whispers of your body, deciphering its language of sensations, and responding with compassion.

It can be as simple as taking a leisurely stroll in nature, feeling the earth beneath your feet and the gentle breeze on your skin. Or it can be an invigorating dance class where you surrender to the rhythm and let your body express its innate grace. Somatic self-care invites you to engage in mindful movement, awakening your senses and reconnecting with the present moment. It's a delightful invitation to explore embodiment, to inhabit your physicality fully. Whether it's through yoga, tai chi, or ecstatic dance, you embrace the joy of movement and celebrate the miracle of your body in motion.

It isn't limited to physical practices alone. It also encompasses the art of self-compassion and self-acceptance. It's about cultivating a nurturing inner dialogue where you speak to yourself with kindness and appreciation. It's about carving out moments of stillness, where you can sink into the embrace of deep relaxation and release any tensions held within your body. It's a radical act of self-love—a celebration of your unique essence and an acknowledgment of the sacredness of your physical form. By engaging in these practices, you create a harmonious union between your body and mind, fostering a sanctuary of well-being within yourself.

So, let your body be your guide, and embark on this enchanting journey of somatic self-care. Dance with the rhythms of life, nurture your body's whispers, and embrace the transformative power of honoring your physical being. In this rhythmic symphony of self-care, you'll discover a profound sense of wholeness and a radiant vitality that permeates every aspect of your existence. And now, using all the tips and tricks that I'll share with you, I encourage you to dig deep and to create a personalized routine that fits for you. It doesn't have to be perfect. It just has to be yours.

When starting out with your somatic self-care routine, it can be quite daunting at first and knowing where to start can feel like you're juggling oranges while trying to walk on a tightrope. What I have found to be helpful is to break it up into three separate aspects: mental, physical, and emotional.

First, check to see which parts of you are most tired, and then you can decide where or with what you want to start. If self-care is something that you've been neglecting for a little while, all of you might feel tired, which is okay. You can start with the place that will feel easiest for you.

Physical: with this, you're checking in with your body and how it's doing. This can look like nourishing your body with:

- quality, balanced meals.
- physically moving your body
- touching yourself tenderly like running your hands all over your body and being grateful for your body and all that it does for you.
- taking a nap
- physical intimacy with a partner or with yourself
- Soaking in a bath
- cuddling a pet

Emotional: these are the things that give your emotions the space to be heard and expressed. You can do this through:

- journaling
- calling a friend or a family member
- meditation
- artwork
- breathwork
- writing poetry

Mental: doing things that stimulate you intellectually—things that give you a bit of a brain break

- reading a new book

- listening to an audiobook or a podcast
- allowing yourself to rest and not to do anything
- playing a game
- Playing sports or going for a walk in nature

Tips for Integrating Somatic Practices Into Daily Life

Making self-care an everyday thing can feel like a daunting thing to do. Especially when we feel like there are a million other things on our plates, things that are more important, but I want to remind you that it doesn't have to be all that complicated or difficult.

Start small: So many of us put pressure to do hours and hours of self-care when just a few minutes a day will do. Stretching just for a few moments while you're at your desk, or doing a little breathing while waiting in the check-out line, will do wonders for you. By taking small steps we make it a lot easier for ourselves to start and keep moving forward.

Make reminders for yourself: If it's not diarized, it's so easy to let it slip; make a note on your calendar: *remember to take care of yourself today or remember to breathe.* These little reminders will make the biggest of differences and make it easier for you to also be more intentional in your practice.

Make it enjoyable: The word 'self' in self-care shows that it's for you, not for anyone else. So just because some influencers enjoyed x, y, and z, doesn't necessarily mean that it will be appealing to you. If you're miserable in your practice, you're likely going to be miserable, which means that you're likely not going to continue with it, but if you like the activities, you'll feel excited about how you're showing up for yourself.

I think that's a more sustainable approach, don't you think?

Do it with others. If you think of doing yoga or going for a walk alone, grab a friend, and do it together, it will help make it a more enjoyable experience.

Be compassionate and patient with yourself. It might take you a bit of time to actually figure out what you like. So, remember not to throw in the towel or give up all too soon. Be kind to yourself, keep cheering on you, and you'll see soon enough you'll find your rhythm and flow.

Self-compassion and Self-Care Practices for Difficult Times

Healing work can be sobering. A deeply profound and transformative experience, Engaging in the process requires a level of introspection, vulnerability, and confronting your own pain or trauma. It is a courageous journey that demands honesty and a willingness to face the sometimes harsh realities of our past.

When embarking on the journey, we may initially be filled with hope and optimism, eagerly anticipating the positive changes that lie ahead. However, as we delve deeper into the layers of our own wounds, we may discover aspects of ourselves that we don't like. It often brings forth buried memories or suppressed emotions that we may have long forgotten or consciously chosen to ignore. It forces us to confront the pain and discomfort that we have been avoiding, and this is something that can be incredibly challenging. It requires us to take responsibility for our own healing. It reminds us that we are the architects of our own lives, and that true healing comes from within, from us. This realization can be both empowering and daunting because it places the onus on us to actively participate in our own healing process. It requires us to acknowledge our own agency and make conscious choices to prioritize our well-being. And I mean, isn't it much easier to cast the blame and place all that responsibility elsewhere in someone else's hands?

But on the hard days, those days where we admit that we don't want to work on ourselves or our healing, we can gently hold ourselves and remind ourselves that, too, is okay and a normal part of the process.

We are only human, susceptible to fluctuations in motivation and energy. We may stumble upon moments when the weight of our experiences feels overwhelming, and the thought of diving into the depths of our emotions becomes daunting. It is in these moments of vulnerability that we must offer ourselves kindness and understanding— recognizing that healing is not a linear path but rather a complex and multifaceted journey.

By embracing the truth that we all have days where we feel resistant to the work required for our healing, we can release the pressure we may put on ourselves to constantly be in a state of growth. We can grant ourselves permission to take a step back, to rest and recharge. It is through accepting and honoring these emotions that we can cultivate a deeper sense of self-compassion and self-acceptance. Embrace the ebb and flow of the healing process, knowing that these moments of pause will pass.

Showing Yourself Self-Compassion

Show up for yourself with kindness, with grace when life becomes difficult—that's when you need it the most. Perhaps you're feeling overwhelmed with a whole lot of emotions, and you don't quite know where to start processing them. More so, you don't really know how to be there for yourself. I'll help you get there:

Start with courage: "This is hard. And I certainly don't know what the future holds for me, but I choose to believe in the fact that mine is a resilient spirit, and I will get back up again.

Follow with curiosity: *"Is there anything that I can learn from all of this? What kinds of valuable messages are my emotions carrying right now?"*

End with grace: "I know that I feel less than adequate right now, but I know that I am smart, resourceful, and have the capacity to build a beautiful life for myself.

Here are a couple of other suggestions:

- Take a moment to acknowledge and validate your suffering. Remember that it is normal to have difficult days and that you deserve kindness and understanding.
- Use comforting and reassuring words, reminding yourself that you are doing your best and that it's okay to struggle.
- Write down your thoughts and feelings in a journal, allowing yourself to express and process your emotions. Use this as an opportunity to offer yourself words of compassion and encouragement.
- Practice a loving-kindness meditation, where you direct well-wishes and love toward yourself. Repeat phrases such as *"May I be happy, may I be healthy, may I be safe, may I live with ease,"* and genuinely wish these things for yourself.
- Reach out to trusted friends, family, or a therapist who can offer support and understanding. Sometimes simply talking about your struggles with someone who listens non-judgmentally can provide

immense relief.

- Remind yourself that it is okay to have hard days and that you are not alone in experiencing them. Cultivate self-acceptance by recognizing that imperfections and setbacks are part of being human.
- Engage in activities that bring comfort and soothe your emotions. This could include listening to calming music, cuddling with a pet, or watching a favorite movie.
- Let go of self-judgment and criticism. Instead of criticizing yourself for your mistakes, treat yourself with kindness and understanding. Try to look at yourself from a different viewpoint. Imagine a friend in your situation and visualize what you might say to them. Remember your strengths. Make a list of your strengths and accomplishments to remind yourself of your worth.
- Take a moment to reflect on things you are grateful for, even on difficult days. Focusing on the positive aspects of your life can help shift your perspective and cultivate self-compassion.

Facing Resistance and Your Inner-Critic

Ah, the inner critic! That little voice inside our heads that loves to chime in and give its unsolicited two cents. It's like having a tiny, relentless backseat driver on the road of self-discovery. Picture this: you're cruising along the highway, eager to explore new horizons and embrace positive change. But just as you gain momentum, there it is—it hops into the passenger seat, armed with a megaphone and a never-ending playlist of doubts and insecurities.

The thing about the inner critic is that it thrives on attention. It feeds off your fears and vulnerabilities, making them grow stronger with each negative thought you entertain. They make us internalize those critical voices from external sources such as societal expectations, past experiences, or comparisons with others. But if we want to reduce the hold that they have on us, it's important to remember that our inner critics are not an accurate reflection of our true worth or potential. They are distorted perceptions that can be reshaped and transformed.

So, today be the person that you need. Your inner critic doesn't and shouldn't get to run the show.

Start by creating awareness around your thoughts. We often get so used to hearing the narratives of our voices that we actually become oblivious to the messages that we are sending to ourselves. Pay attention to what you're thinking and recognize that just because you're thinking something, it does not necessarily mean that it is true.

Let go of the rumination. When we make mistakes or when we've had bad days, it's so easy to want to replay the events of that day over and over in our heads., but repeatedly reminding ourselves of those situations doesn't fix anything; it only makes matters worse and won't solve the problem. Distract yourself with an activity; it might stop the thoughts from spiraling out of control.

What advice would you give to a friend? "You're hopeless," "You're weak," "You're a basket case." Are these things that you would say to a friend? I am guessing that the answer is no. So, don't speak to yourself like that. Applying the same race and encouragement that you give to others to your own situation, you also deserve that much, don't you think?

Reframe the statements that you share with yourself. Turn the pessimistic thoughts into something more real. If you find yourself constantly saying things like: "w*help, it seems to me like I am always so helpless.*" change that to "*Some days are harder than others, but I really do like to believe that I am doing alright.*" and that's because you really are.

Your inner dialogue is going to fuel your growth, or it's going to push you back a lot. Being too harsh on yourself might altogether make you want to give up on yourself, but you, so tame that inner voice, healing does, after all, come when we are willing to give ourselves the grace we need to make it through the tough times.

7

The Importance of Safety and Boundaries in Somatic Therapy

"Setting boundaries is not about building walls or separating ourselves from others. It's about creating a safe and sacred space within which we can grow, flourish, and thrive."

— CHER HAMPTON

Boundaries, an essential aspect of relationships, are not just walls to keep others out but rather a delineation of our personal space, values, and emotional health. They are the invisible lines that define the contours of our individuality. When respected, they nurture our self-esteem, promoting a healthy interplay between independence and interdependence. They help us preserve the love within us by ensuring that our emotional reservoir is not depleted. This becomes especially crucial when relationships face trials and transformations or even when they end.

In the complex weave of human relationships, some threads may unravel, leading to the reality of goodbye. This farewell can be fraught with a myriad of emotions - pain, regret, relief, and even a sense of liberation. It is during these times that good boundaries come to the forefront as our protectors. They remind us that our self-worth is not tied to the longevity of our relationships but lies within the authenticity of our interactions and the lessons we glean from them.

Good boundaries also safeguard our ability to love. They prevent us from losing ourselves in relationships that no longer serve us, ensuring that we have the emotional energy to invest in new relationships or deepen existing ones. They give us the resilience to say goodbye, not as an end, but as a new beginning.

So, while it may be difficult to accept the reality of goodbye, it is through these goodbyes that we often discover our true selves. Boundaries allow us to embrace these transitions with grace and courage, safe in the knowledge that our ability to love remains undiminished. They teach us that it is okay to move on, to preserve the love within us, and to continue our journey with a heart open to new relationships and experiences. In this sense, boundaries are not constraints but catalysts for growth, fueling our capacity to love and be loved in return.

Setting Boundaries for Self-Protection and Healing

Good boundaries matter, too, in somatic work. Why? Because the body does its best healing work when it feels safe.

Our nervous systems are constantly asking us, *"Is it safe? Is it safe enough to rest? Is it safe enough to surrender? Is it safe enough to be fully present in this moment, in this body, in this breath?"*

When we're working on healing our bodies, it's so important that we feel safe and secure in order to allow our bodies to do their best healing work.

Our nervous systems are constantly asking us if it's safe to rest, to surrender, to be present in our bodies and our breath. These are all essential aspects of somatic work, but we can't fully engage in them if we don't feel safe. If we don't have boundaries in place, we might not feel safe enough to fully let go and allow ourselves to heal.

Setting boundaries is a form of self-protection, and it allows us to establish a clear space for our healing work to take place. When we set boundaries, we're letting ourselves and others know what we need in order to feel safe and supported. This might look like setting clear limits around physical touch, verbal language, or emotional sharing.

Without boundaries, we might find ourselves feeling overwhelmed, triggered, or re-traumatized during somatic work. But when we establish healthy boundaries, we create a space where we can feel secure enough to open ourselves up to the healing process.

It's important to remember that boundaries aren't just about saying "no" to things that make us feel uncomfortable. They're also about saying "yes" to things that nourish and support us. So, for example, setting a boundary around not discussing certain topics might allow you to feel more comfortable exploring other aspects of your healing journey.

Tips on setting boundaries with someone you trust:

- Before you meet with them, take some time to think about what your boundaries are. This might include things like your comfort level with physical touch, the types of language or topics you're comfortable discussing, or the pace at which you'd like to progress through your healing work.

- It's important to communicate your boundaries clearly and directly. Be honest and upfront about your needs and preferences, and don't be afraid to speak up if something doesn't feel right to you.

- If someone suggests something that doesn't feel right to you, don't hesitate to say no. Remember, it's your body and your healing process, so you get to set the pace and direction of your work.

- If you're struggling to set boundaries or communicate your needs, don't hesitate to seek support from someone you trust. This could be a friend or family member.

- Boundaries can shift and change over time as we grow and heal. It's important to revisit your boundaries regularly and adjust them as needed. Don't be afraid to have an open and ongoing conversation with yourself, moments of reflection where you acknowledge what's working and what's not.

Tips on Setting Boundaries With Yourself:

Setting boundaries with ourselves in our healing work can be just as important as setting boundaries with others.

- Take some time to identify your goals for your healing work. What are you hoping to achieve? What do you need to do to get there? This will help you set a clear direction for your work.

- Be honest with yourself about what you can realistically achieve in a given amount of time. Don't set yourself up for failure by expecting too much too soon.

- Healing takes time, and it's important to be patient and compassionate with yourself as you navigate the ups and downs of the process. Remember that you're doing the best you can and that every step forward is progress.

- Pay attention to your body and its needs. If you're feeling tired or overwhelmed, take a break. If you're feeling stuck, try a different approach. Trust yourself and your instincts.
- Take time to celebrate your progress, no matter how small. Acknowledge the work you've done and the progress you've made. This will help you stay motivated and focused on your goals.
- When we set our boundaries, we feel safe enough to ask for help. To tell the truth, safe enough to be messy and imperfect. Remember that.

Cultivating a Sense of Safety and Trust in the Body

We can slowly, gently, and tenderly teach our bodies that the unfamiliar doesn't feel unsafe. Unfamiliar can be beautiful. Magical. Unfamiliar can be glorious. Unfamiliar can be healing.

Learning to cultivate a sense of safety and trust in the body is a powerful act of self-love. It's a process of developing a positive relationship with the self, a relationship that allows us to move through the world with less fear and more openness.

Our bodies often carry the weight of past traumas, experiences that have left us feeling unsafe and disconnected. These experiences can cause us to withdraw and become closed off to new experiences. But it's possible to create new pathways in the body, pathways that lead to a more open and trusting relationship with ourselves and the world around us.

One way to do this is to slowly, gently, and tenderly teach our bodies that the unfamiliar doesn't have to feel unsafe. We can begin by practicing self-compassion and self-care, paying attention to our bodies' needs, and responding with kindness and compassion. We can also work with our thoughts, using positive affirmations and visualizations to counteract negative beliefs and patterns that may be holding us back.

As we begin to build trust and safety in ourselves, we can also start to explore new experiences and sensations. This might mean trying new foods, exploring new hobbies or interests, or simply spending time in unfamiliar environments. As we do this, we can remind ourselves that unfamiliarity doesn't have to be scary or overwhelming. Unfamiliar can be beautiful. Magical. Glorious. And, perhaps most importantly, being unfamiliar can be safe.

This process of learning to cultivate safety and trust in the body is not always easy, but it is deeply rewarding. It allows us to let go of old patterns and beliefs that no longer serve us and to embrace new possibilities and experiences with open arms. It also opens the door to deeper, more meaningful connections with ourselves and with others. So, take a deep breath, and start the journey of learning to trust your body and all that it is capable of. You may be surprised by what you find. This is how you do it:

Rest is anything that makes our nervous systems feel safe enough to switch off our stress responses to our minds and bodies so that we can move into a state. By slowing down and resting and being intentional about wanting to be fully present in our lives, we quietly participate in creating a loving world for ourselves.

Oh, and here's another thing, rest is and can be more than taking naps. It can look like stretching, nourishing food, or mindful movement.

It's mental rest too—which is essentially any non-thinking activity: baking, painting. Gardening and single-tasking.

There's emotional rest, too: journalling, going to therapy, sharing rather than suppressing.

Social rest: finding solace in solitude or intimacy. It's a sense of community.

Sensory rest is in silence, listening to relaxing music, and wearing comfortable clothing and cozy socks.

Spiritual rest is choosing to focus on what is true for you. It's prayer, pottery, yoga, and energetic alignment.

Playful rest is anything that makes you feel carefree and fun.

Not done yet, there's ecological rest—caring for your houseplants or growing your own garden, it's birdwatching, swimming out in the will.

Rest is a lot of things. You can match the kind of rest with the type of unease or stress that you're experiencing. For example, if you've been in a noisy environment, you can offer yourself sensory rest as a gentle and loving reminder. At the end of the day, it's all about asking what stress I am experiencing today. What kind of rest would be helpful right now?

Give your body an identity of its own. So often, we wage wars with our bodies because we view them only as objects. Giving your body its own identity requires shifting the way you view it. Rather than seeing your body as a mere object, try to view it as a living entity with its own unique qualities and functions. Think of it as a partner in your journey through life, with its own personality and needs.

Here are some ways you can start to do that:

- **Personalize it**: Give your body a name, a personality, and even a story. This can help to humanize it and make it feel more tangible.
- **Listen to its signals**: Pay attention to what your body is telling you. When you feel hungry, tired, or sore, respond with nourishment, rest, and care.
- **Practice self-compassion**: Don't be too hard on yourself when your body doesn't perform exactly how you want it to. Instead, show yourself self-compassion, acknowledging that your body is doing the best it can.
- **Be grateful**: Appreciate your body for all the things it does for you every day, like allowing you to breathe, move, and experience the world.

Another key factor in learning to trust your body is **developing an understanding of how your body reacts to different situations**. Understanding your body's stress response, for example, can help you identify when you're feeling anxious or overwhelmed and take the steps needed to manage those feelings. On the other hand, listening to your body's cues during exercise can help you avoid injury and push yourself to reach your fitness goals.

Trust doesn't come easily, especially when it comes to our bodies. Society puts so much pressure on us to look a certain way, perform at a high level, and attain a specific level of fitness. Still, learning to trust your body means developing a better understanding of what it can and can't do and accepting it for what it is. Celebrate your body for its uniqueness, nurture it with healthy decisions, and trust it to carry you through life's ups and downs.

Recognizing and Addressing Triggers and Challenges in Somatic Work

It's important to acknowledge that triggers and boundaries are interconnected concepts that play a crucial role in understanding and addressing emotional and physiological responses in individuals. Triggers are events or stimuli that elicit strong emotional or physiological responses, often stemming from past traumatic experiences or deeply ingrained patterns of behavior. Boundaries, on the other hand, are the limits we set to protect ourselves and maintain emotional well-being. By recognizing and navigating our triggers while establishing and maintaining healthy boundaries, we can create a safe and supportive environment for healing and personal growth.

Just like landmines, triggers are hidden beneath the surface, waiting to be activated. When someone steps on a landmine, it detonates and causes an explosion. So, when a trigger is activated, it sets off a powerful reaction within your nervous system.

Now let's delve into triggers in the context of somatic work. Somatic work involves close proximity making it easier for certain things to act as triggers, leading to strong bodily sensations or emotional responses. Here are a couple of examples:

Physical touch: For some individuals, physical touch can be a trigger. This might be due to past experiences of abuse or trauma. When these individuals encounter certain types of touch, it can activate a fight-or-flight response, causing them to feel anxious, unsafe, or even re-

116

experience traumatic memories.

Loud noises: Loud noises can be triggers for people who have experienced traumatic events associated with loud sounds. These individuals might have been exposed to explosions, gunshots, or other violent incidents. When they encounter loud noises in the present, it can trigger a fear response, causing heightened anxiety, hypervigilance, or a sense of impending danger.

Intense emotions: Sometimes, strong emotions themselves can act as triggers. For instance, someone who has experienced a traumatic event might find that feeling anger or sadness triggers memories or sensations associated with that event. This can lead to an overwhelming emotional response, including panic or dissociation.

It's important to note that triggers can be highly individualized, and what triggers one person may not affect another in the same way. Additionally, triggers can be complex and can vary in intensity depending on a person's current state of mind, level of stress, or other contextual factors.

Understanding triggers is a crucial part of somatic work because it allows individuals to recognize when they are being activated and provides an opportunity to explore and heal the underlying causes.

Practical Tips for Learning to Manage Your Triggers

A note on healing our triggers: when I first embarked on my healing journey, I had this false idea that there would come a day when I wouldn't be triggered anymore and all those memories of the things in the past that hurt me, wouldn't come back to hurt me anymore. Time and time again, I got triggered, and each time that would happen, I would get completely heartbroken, disappointed, and almost give up completely. But then I realized that perhaps, that was a rather incorrect approach to take. I didn't need to focus on erasing the memories completely. But rather on incorporating them into my whole self, accepting them, and being conscious of them.

- Pay attention to your body and emotions to identify when you're being triggered. Notice any physical sensations or changes in mood or behavior that indicate a trigger is being activated.
- Develop a safety plan that outlines strategies and coping mechanisms to use when triggered. This can include self-soothing techniques, supportive affirmations, or engaging in activities that bring you comfort and calm.
- Identify internal and external resources that can provide support when triggered. Internal resources might include positive memories or personal strengths, while external resources can be supportive relationships, safe spaces, or calming activities.
- Gradually expose yourself to triggers in a controlled and safe environment. This can help desensitize your response over time. However, it's crucial to work with a therapist who can guide and support you through this process.
- Develop coping strategies: Explore and practice coping strategies that help regulate your emotions and manage the physiological response to triggers. This might include breathing exercises, visualization techniques that we talked about earlier on in the book, or objects like stress balls or fidget spinners.

I Want You to Remember About Your Triggers

You're not broken or damaged beyond, you're a work in progress, and that's a rather beautiful thing. Here are a final few reminders I want you to keep in mind:

- Triggers are a natural part of the human experience. We all have things that can set us off, and it's important to remember that there's nothing wrong with us for having them.
- Triggers can be an opportunity for growth. When we understand what triggers us and why, we can start to heal and work through those wounds.
- Triggers can help us to set boundaries. When we know what situations or people trigger us, we can take steps to protect ourselves and create healthier boundaries.
- Triggers can be managed with the right tools and support. Whether it's therapy, mindfulness, or other self-care practices, there are ways to manage and cope with triggers so that they have less power over us.
- Triggers don't define us. While they can be intense and overwhelming, our triggers are just one small part of who we are as individuals.
- Triggers can bring us closer to others. When we share our triggers with trusted loved ones or seek support from a therapist, we create opportunities for deeper connection and understanding.
- Triggers are a reminder that we're human. We're all imperfect, and triggers can be a reminder of that. However, with self-compassion and self-love, we can learn to accept and embrace our triggers as an essential part of our journey toward healing and growth.

Interactive Exercise: Identifying Your Triggers

Let's get interactive and identify some of your triggers! I've created

119

this exercise for you to become more aware of what sets you off and how to manage those triggers when they arise.

First, take a few deep breaths and think of a recent situation where you felt triggered. It might have been a disagreement with someone or a stressful moment at work or school. Whatever it was, just picture it in your mind without judging yourself or anyone else involved.

Now, read through the list of common triggers below and see which ones resonate with you. You don't have to check all of them, just the ones that feel relevant to your experience.

- criticism or rejection
- feeling out of control
- feeling overwhelmed
- feeling unsupported or unappreciated
- feeling disrespected or betrayed
- feeling judged or misunderstood
- feeling helpless or powerless
- feeling abandoned or ignored

Grab a piece of paper or a notebook and write down your triggers. Then take a moment to acknowledge how each one impacts you. Do you feel upset, anxious, frustrated, or something else? How do your triggers affect your relationships and your daily life?

Now it's time to empower yourself! Remember that you have the ability to manage your triggers and respond to them in a healthy way. Start by making a plan for how to react the next time you face one of your triggers. Your plan could include things like taking a walk, talking to a trusted friend, or practicing deep breathing exercises.

Remember to be gentle with yourself as you navigate this process; it's going to be hard and take a lot from you mentally and emotionally, but just hold on to the reminder that it is the path toward a brighter tomorrow, a happier you.

I must say, I'm feeling a whirlwind of emotions! But as they say, it's all part of the journey to self-improvement. And in the upcoming chapter, we'll finally get to the bottom of that burning question that's been on your mind: Can self-help truly take us on the healing journey we need? I'm just as eager as you are to find out, so let's turn that page and discover the answer together!

8

Extra Somatic Exercises

"The joy of progress is progress."

— UNKNOWN

This journey with you has been incredible so far. Thank you for being here. And more so, thank you for the bravery that you are showing in unpacking your own experiences; that's hardly the easiest of things to do. So, I want you to remember progress isn't just a fleeting feeling; it's a sign that you genuinely are getting somewhere, a better place. So, focus on that, focus on the enjoyment of feeling. When you focus on the positive feelings more than you do the negative ones, you're more likely to keep yourself moving forward.

So, I want you to think of this chapter as a bonus, one with useful tips and suggestions for somatic exercises that you can incorporate along with the other exercises that we discussed and talked about in this book.

Affirmations

As we said in the beginning, affirmations are like gentle, encouraging whispers that you can use to fill the spaces in your heart that are ridden with the grief, the uncertainty, and the messiness of the healing journey. So here are a few that I have compiled for you. Take whichever ones you need, and as you say them, place your hands on your heart, breathe, and hold on to the reminder that you will get through this.

Affirmations for Uncertainty

- I know that this feels rather hard right now, and it feels like there's no silver lining, but I know that I am strong enough to make my way.
- I believe in my own resilience and courage will help me get through this.
- I release fear and embrace the unknown as an opportunity for growth.
- I am worthy of a life that is filled with happiness and peace.
- I deserve to let go of past pain and embrace a future filled with love and joy.
- In choosing momentary discomfort, I am creating a strong foundation of self-love and self-acceptance.
- I am open to receiving healing energy from the universe.
- I am releasing all negative emotions and making space for love and positivity in my life.
- I am transforming into a more authentic and empowered version of myself.
- The past does not define me, and I am creating a bright future for myself.
- I let go of guilt and forgive myself for any perceived mistakes or

shortcomings.
- Grace and ease find me effortlessly, even in the midst of uncertainty.
- I trust in the process of healing and have faith in my ability to recover.
- I am resilient and can bounce back from any emotional setbacks.
- I will be gentle with myself as I navigate the uncertainties of my healing journey.
- I have the power to create my own happiness and rewrite my story.

Affirmations for Making Space for Joy

- I am an amalgamation of all the things that light up my soul and make me glow when I talk about them.
- Joy is capable of finding me without much effort and with so much ease.
- I don't have to wait for joy to follow and find me; I'm choosing to intentionally chase after it, and when I find it. I'll hold on as tightly as I can.
- I will look for the good in this day.
- I will slow down, pause and savor each moment as it comes.
- I will be honest but still kind to myself.
- I will make today as beautiful as I can—whatever that looks like.
- This story of my life is written with grace, gratitude, and a whole lot of goodness.
- This story of mine is written with joy, peace, and presence.
- My heart is open to experiencing the joys, beauties, and the gift of small things.
- With every challenge and upheaval comes the chance to decide who we want to be and what we want our lives to be about—joy is what I choose those to be.

Affirmations for Choosing Peace

- Everything that I will do today will be in alignment with my highest self. I deserve to be without the energies of my experiences weighing down on me.
- I am choosing peace, which also means that I am working on nurturing self-trust and confidence so that I can go after all the things that I want. This right here is healing, and I'm going full force after it.
- I am going to work on reminding myself before going into any situation that I can 100% be myself. No one or no circumstance gets to choose that for me.
- Protecting my ease means that I get to leave any situation at any given time if it is no longer serving my peace. May I hold on to the truth in those words
- I will take it day by day and be grateful for the little things, and not stress too much over what I can't control.
- I am a remarkable person and I bring love and understanding into all spaces.
- I know that I am capable enough to confidently embrace the change that comes from an unknown future.
- I can trust that everything is happening for my highest and for the best.
- I choose to be surrounded by those who bring me peace, love, and support.

A Guided Meditation for Cultivating Peace

Welcome to this moment dedicated to cultivating a sense of inner peace and serenity. Whether you're in a quiet room, a peaceful garden, or simply in the comfort of your own mind, let's journey together into a realm of calm and tranquility.

1. Start by finding a comfortable position. It could be sitting, lying down, or even standing. The goal is to be comfortable but alert. If you're sitting, try to keep your spine upright yet relaxed. If lying down, allow your body to sink into the support beneath you.

2. Now, gently close your eyes. As you do so, imagine the world outside quieting down, its noise and chaos fading into the distance, replaced with a comforting silence.

3. Let's take a deep breath, drawing in peace, calmness, and serenity. Notice the cool air entering your nostrils, filling your lungs completely. Hold it for a moment... and then release. As you exhale, imagine letting go of any tension, stress, or discomfort. Repeat this a few times, encouraging your body to relax deeper with every exhale.

4. Now, visualize a beautiful, serene place. This could be a quiet beach with calm waves, a lush forest with gentle leaves rustling, or perhaps a tranquil meadow under a clear blue sky. This is your sanctuary of peace, your inner haven.

5. In this peaceful landscape, imagine a gentle, soothing light shining down from above. This light represents peace, calm, and tranquility. As it touches your skin, feel it bringing warmth and serenity to your body, beginning from the top of your head and slowly spreading to your feet. Every cell it touches is bathed in peace and tranquility.

6. With each breath, this light becomes brighter, more vibrant. It's soothing, healing, and calming. It's absorbing any stress, tension, or worries you might have. They're being drawn up and out of your body, evaporating into the air, leaving only peace behind.

7. Breathe in this light, this peace. Allow it to fill every part of you, not just your physical body but also your emotions, your thoughts,

and your spirit. Each breath in is peace; each breath out is released.

8. Now, imagine this light expanding outwards, touching everything in its path, spreading peace and tranquility all around you. Your surroundings, your town, and your world is gradually being bathed in this peaceful light.

9. Spend some time in this peaceful state, enjoying the sensation of tranquility, calmness, and serenity. This is your inner peace, your sanctuary that you can return to any time you wish.

10. As we start to draw this meditation to a close, remember this sense of peace you've cultivated today. It's always within you, waiting to be tapped into. All you need to do is close your eyes and breathe.

11. Take a few more deep, intentional breaths. Feel your body and mind reconnecting with the space around you. Gently wiggle your fingers and toes, bringing a gentle movement back into your body. When you're ready, slowly, gently open your eyes.

12. Remember, peace is not a destination but a journey that you can gently ease yourself into.

A practical tip: another great exercise that you can try is to keep a journal alongside you as you repeat these affirmations, and then, using them as inspiration, you can create a few of your own. Once you've found the ones that resonate the most with you, put them on sticky notes or place them in an area that you frequent; that way, you'll always have a gentle reminder—or two, and even three to remind you of the remarkable power that you wield!

Peaceful Recharge: A Self-Soothing Exercise for Inner Calm

Step 1: Find a quiet, comfortable space

Create a peaceful environment by finding a quiet space where you won't be disturbed, and make sure you're sitting or lying down in a comfortable position. Take a deep breath and settle into your body.

Step 2: Focus on your breath

Close your eyes and take a few deep breaths to calm down. Breathe in deeply through your nose and exhale through your mouth, slowly and focused. Imagine the air flowing into your lungs and filling your body with fresh oxygen and energy.

Step 3: Use your senses to ground yourself

Take a moment to use your senses to ground yourself in the present moment. Start by focusing on what you can see, hear, smell, and feel. Take note of your surroundings, like the color of the walls, the sounds of any birds chirping outside, the smell of fresh air or essential oils, and the sensation of your skin against your clothing or the surface you're sitting or lying on.

Step 4: Visualize a safe place

Think of a place where you feel peaceful and safe. It could be a beach, a forest, a mountain, or a cozy room at home. Imagine yourself there, surrounded by the sights, smells, and sounds of your safe place. Allow yourself to be fully immersed in this moment and feel the comfort of the space.

Step 5: Practice progressive muscle relaxation

Focus on different parts of your body one by one. Starting from your toes, tighten and release each muscle group as you breathe deeply. Once you have gone through every muscle group, repeat the process, and let your body release any tension with each exhale.

Step 6: Affirm, Affirm, Affirm

Repeat positive affirmations to yourself. Affirmations can be personal to you, but must be gentle and soothing. Examples may include statements such as "I am safe," or "I am loved," or anything that will remind you of your true value.

Step 7: Close with gratitude

Finish your self-soothing exercise by feeling grateful for your body, your mind, and your ability to take time for yourself. Take a deep belly breath and slowly open your eyes. Stretch out your limbs, give yourself an internal hug, and release yourself into your surroundings, feeling at peace.

Remember, this self-soothing exercise can be practiced as often as needed. Each time you do it, you will become more relaxed and in tune with your body. Enjoy the process, and let yourself experience the benefits of a calm, centered mind.

Recalling Kindness: A Somatic Experiencing Exercise

In this exercise, you will explore the feeling of kindness and use our body's natural ability to regulate and settle to become more familiar with this sensation again.

1. To begin, find a comfortable position, either sitting or lying down and take a deep breath, allowing yourself to settle into your body and the present moment. Notice any sensations in your body

without trying to change them or judge them.

2. Now, bring to mind a time when someone showed you kindness. It could be something as simple as a smile from a stranger or a kind word from a friend. Allow the memory to become vivid in your mind, and notice how your body responds to this feeling of kindness.

3. Perhaps you feel a warmth in your chest or an easing of tension in your shoulders. Maybe you notice a softening in your belly or a gentle tingling in your hands. Whatever sensations you experience, allow them to be there and simply observe them.

4. Now, take a deep breath and invite that feeling of kindness to spread throughout your body. Imagine it flowing from the top of your head to the tips of your toes like a warm, comforting blanket. Notice any internal resistance to this sensation and gently invite yourself to stay with it.

5. As you continue to breathe deeply, you may notice that the feeling of kindness becomes more familiar and easier to access. Allow yourself to bask in this sensation, knowing that you can return to it whenever you need to.

6. When you feel ready, take a deep breath and slowly open your eyes. Notice any differences in how you feel compared to when you started this exercise. Perhaps you feel more relaxed, calmer, or more connected to your body.

Remember, you can return to this exercise whenever you need a reminder of the power of kindness and how it can help you regulate your nervous system.

Knowing When It's Time to Ask For Help

Okay, so let's say you've been on this self-help train for some time, and somewhere along the way, you realize that something is amiss. You feel unsettled by the realization that the techniques you've been using aren't quite doing the trick anymore. You're experiencing new symptoms, feeling stuck, or nothing seems to bring you the relief you so desperately need. This can be a frustrating and overwhelming experience, but it's important to recognize that knowing when it's time to ask for help is a critical component of self-help somatic therapy. The reality is that self-help is not always sufficient. Those moments where the thought of asking for help makes you feel powerless, but you go ahead and do it, either way, is an incredible act of courage. Don't take that too lightly. It's important to remember that seeking help does not mean giving up. Rather, it's acknowledging that self-help is just one piece of the puzzle, and that additional support may be needed to get all the other pieces to connect with one another.

Here are some signs to look out for as an indication that it might be time to ask for help.

- **Feeling overwhelmed**: If you find yourself constantly feeling overwhelmed by your emotions, thoughts, or daily life, it could be a sign that self-help methods aren't providing enough relief.
- **Persistent or worsening symptoms**: If your symptoms, whether physical or psychological, persist or worsen despite your self-help efforts, it might be time to explore other avenues of support.
- **Interference with daily functioning**: When your struggles start interfering with your ability to function in your personal or professional life, it's a clear indication that you might need additional help.

- **Recurring patterns or unresolved issues**: If you notice recurring patterns or unresolved issues that you can't seem to address effectively on your own, it could be a sign that deeper exploration is needed. Sometimes, professional guidance can help you uncover underlying causes or develop more effective strategies for dealing with these challenges.
- **Lack of progress or plateau**: Despite your best efforts in self-help and somatic therapy, you may reach a point where you feel stuck or like you're not making progress. This can be frustrating and demotivating.

Few Final Tips

Embrace vulnerability, even when it's hard. Allow yourself to be seen and heard. Remember, it's through vulnerability that true healing and growth can take place.

Remember, too, that healing is about practicing unconditional acceptance of yourself, especially those parts that you feel are the hardest to love.

Be realistic about your expectations. Healing is a journey that requires patience and commitment. Set realistic expectations for yourself and understand that progress may come in small steps. Celebrate each milestone along the way.

The effectiveness of somatic therapy relies on honesty and a lack of judgment, so allow yourself to explore the journey at a pace that is natural to you.

Approach it with an open mind and a willingness to explore new perspectives. Be open to challenging your beliefs and assumptions, as this can lead to deeper self-awareness and personal growth.

Take ownership of your journey. Remember that healing is ultimately about empowering yourself. Take ownership of your own healing journey and actively participate in the process.

Take the time to research and find methods that are a good fit for your needs and goals. Trust your instincts and prioritize building that relationship of trust with yourself.

A great life is out there waiting for you. A great, big, beautiful life where you no longer have and get to be defined by things of the past, things that were out of and beyond your control. To you, a beautiful life calls. One where you realize that joy has always been a part of the equation. A life where you come to understand and see that it was never really about how you experience the world but rather how you allow the world to experience you. So go out there and allow yourself to heal and exist as boldly as you can.

Conclusion

"Allow the body to discharge its bound energy and embrace what is, the organism's natural self regulation. Relax. Breathe."

— SAKTI ROSE

This version of you is healing, growing, and will still make mistakes. You have so much to offer and are deserving of love. You are an inspiration to others. You are one step closer and should be so proud of how far you've come.

Let us recap the key points that will empower and guide us as we continue to navigate our personal growth:

Somatic therapy reminds us that our bodies hold deep wisdom and profound truths. It teaches us to listen intently to the gentle whispers and powerful messages our bodies convey. By attuning ourselves to these bodily sensations, we unlock a wellspring of insights that lead us toward healing and wholeness.

Through somatic therapy, we learn to identify and understand our triggers. These triggers act as signposts, revealing wounds and unresolved emotions that reside within us. By acknowledging and exploring these triggers with compassion, we can unravel the roots of our pain and begin the process of healing.

Somatic therapy invites us to fully embrace our embodied experience. It encourages us to be present in our bodies, to inhabit each breath, sensation, and movement. By cultivating this mindful connection, we tap into a well of resilience, strength, and self-awareness that propels us forward on our healing journey.

In our pursuit of self-healing, somatic therapy teaches us the transformative power of self-compassion. It reminds us to treat ourselves with kindness, gentleness, and understanding. By extending this compassion to our wounded selves, we create a safe and nurturing environment for healing to unfold.

Somatic therapy emphasizes the interconnectedness of our mind, body, and spirit. It encourages us to honor and integrate these aspects of ourselves, recognizing that true healing occurs when we address the whole person. By fostering harmony and balance within ourselves, we embark on a holistic journey of self-rediscovery and growth.

This is it. The end, but not so much the end in so many words. I know that for so many of you, this book will be exactly what you need, and for others, it might just be a starting place for your healing journey. Whatever the case may be, I hope you can rest on the reminder that I am rooting for you forever and always. The help you need is never too far away, and you don't have to feel ashamed about the need to ask for help.

As you journey forward, remember that healing is not a linear process, and there will be ups and downs along the way. It takes courage to confront past traumas and work through them. But know that every step you take, no matter how small, brings you closer to a healthier and happier you.

Somatic therapy is a powerful tool, but it is just one of many resources available to you. Remember to utilize other forms of therapy, self-care practices, and support from loved ones as needed.

As you close this book and continue on your journey, I hope you carry with you the knowledge that you are not alone, and that healing is possible. May you find peace, comfort, and strength in your path ahead, knowing that I am with you every step of the way.

BONUS: Your Free Gift

I'm only offering this bonus for FREE to my readers. This is a way of saying thanks for your purchase. In this gift, you will find a course with extra tools to start your inner journey.

The Personality Development Wisdom Course

Master the Art of Becoming the Best Version of Yourself for Ultimate Succes and Growth!

Inside this course, you will find:

1. Personality Development - An Overview
2. How to Transform Yourself into a Better Version
3. How To Improve Your Body Language
4. How to Boost Up Your Self-Confidence, Self-Esteem, and Motivation
5. Best Tips to Overcome Procrastination
6. The Power of Positive Thinking
7. How to Improve Your Workplace Wellness
8. How to Enhance Your Softskill
9. Learn and Practice the Art of Work-Life Balance
10. How to Deal With Failures
11. How to Manage and Overcome Your Fears
12. Best Ways to Deal With Difficult People
13. Stress and Energy Management
14. How to Have a Productive Day
15. Bonus 1 - Cheat Sheet
16. Bonus 2 - Mind Map
17. Bonus 3 - Top Resource Report
18. Bonus 4 - 10 Extra Articles

To receive this extra **bonus,** go to: https://booksforbetterlife.com/somatic-therapy-handbook

Or scan the QR code:

BONUS: YOUR FREE GIFT

Thank You!

I really appreciate you for purchasing my book!

You had the chance to pick a lot of other books, but you chose this one.

So, **thank you so much** for purchasing this book and reading it to the very last page! I hope that I was able to help you in your healing process, as my goal is to help as many people as possible!

Before you close the book, I want to ask for **a small favor**. Would you please consider *leaving an honest review* about the book? **This would be really helpful for me**, as I'm an independent author and posting reviews is the best and easiest way to support me.

The feedback you provide will help me so I can continue selling, improving, and writing books. **It will mean the world to me to hear from you!**

Go to my book and scroll down (https://mybook.to/somatic-therapy), or scan the QR code to leave a review:

THANK YOU!

Amazon US <— —> Amazon UK

Amazon CA <— —> Rest of the World

References

Quote Fancy. (n.d.). *Naomi Judd Quote: Your body hears everything your mind says.*

Schuldt, W. (2022). *Grounding techniques.* Therapist Aid.

Silva, L. (2022, December 5). *What is somatic therapy?* Forbes Health.

Torres, E. (2021, June 9). *Can somatic therapy exercises prevent anxiety attacks?* Lead Grow Develop.

Wright, S. (2021, November 8). *Trauma triggers: How to identify and overcome triggers.* Psych Central.

Made in the USA
Middletown, DE
14 October 2023

40780692R00092